To Young Harris College

Bruce Parrish '61

This may be the most honest book ever produced about professional football. It provides a new perspective on America's favorite spectator sport.

Football is energy. Football is emotion. *A Game of Passion* focuses on these essential components. It depicts the joy, the suffering, and the excitement of pro football. It captures the emotional intensity of the game as reflected in the men who play it.

A Game of Passion is a 256-page photographic study of the men of professional football. More than 150 black and white photographs—most of which were taken especially for this book—create an intimate portrait of the game as the players and coaches see it. Each photograph captures a special moment, a special feeling that says something important about the sport of professional football and its players.

Each of the photographers represented in this book has distinguished himself as a creative talent who combines the technical skill and knowledge of photography with an understanding of and sensitivity to pro football.

The photographers' works are accompanied by the prologue and epilogue of Ray Bradbury, one of America's finest writers, and the moving and knowledgeable text of Bob Oates, Jr.

"There is much to be said for the view that Ray Bradbury is in a school by himself," wrote Robert Kirsch in the *Los Angeles Times*. "Prolific, endlessly creative, an explorer of all forms—from poetry to drama, film to novel, short stories to essays—involved and committed, prophetic and visionary, Bradbury comes close to being, in every sense of the word, an original."

Bradbury's numerous works include *Dandelion Wine, Fahrenheit 451, The Illustrated Man,* and *The Martian Chronicles.* Born in Waukegan, Illinois, he grew up in Los Angeles and lives there with his wife and four daughters.

Bob Oates, Jr. graduated summa cum laude and Phi Beta Kappa from the University of Southern California and received a Master's degree in American History from UCLA.

He has written or edited four books on professional football, including *The First 50 Years,* the *Story of the National Football League,* and *Joe Namath: A Matter of Style.*

He is at work on a biography of the Maharishi Mahesh Yogi, the founder of Transcendental Meditation.

a Game of Passion

"Football is many things, but mostly it is a game of passion."

Vince Lombardi

a Game of Passion

Prologue and Epilogue by Ray Bradbury

Text by Bob Oates, Jr.

Photographers

James F. Flores

Rod Hanna

Ross Lewis

Peter Read Miller

M. V. Rubio

Herb Weitman

Michael Zagaris

Designed by David Boss

A National Football League Book

Distributed by Charles Scribner's Sons, New York

A Game of Passion
A National Football League Book
Prepared by National Football League
Properties, Inc. Creative Services Division
Publisher: David Boss
Editor: John Wiebusch
Executive Director: Jack Wrobbel
Managing Editor: Tom Bennett
Associate Editors: Tom Patty, Rick Smith
Editorial Staff: Patricia Cross, Earlene Doran
Associate Designer: Amy Yutani
Production Manager: Patrick McKee
Production Staff: Rob Meneilly,
Kathleen Oldenburg, Jere Wright
Administrative Staff: Dee Gregory, Muriel Lorenz
Hand lettering by Harry Jacobs

Library of Congress Catalog Card Number: 75-15470
ISBN 0-684-14462-x
First Printing 1975
Printed in the United States of America

#

"May our fields become sacred places."

Sherwood Anderson

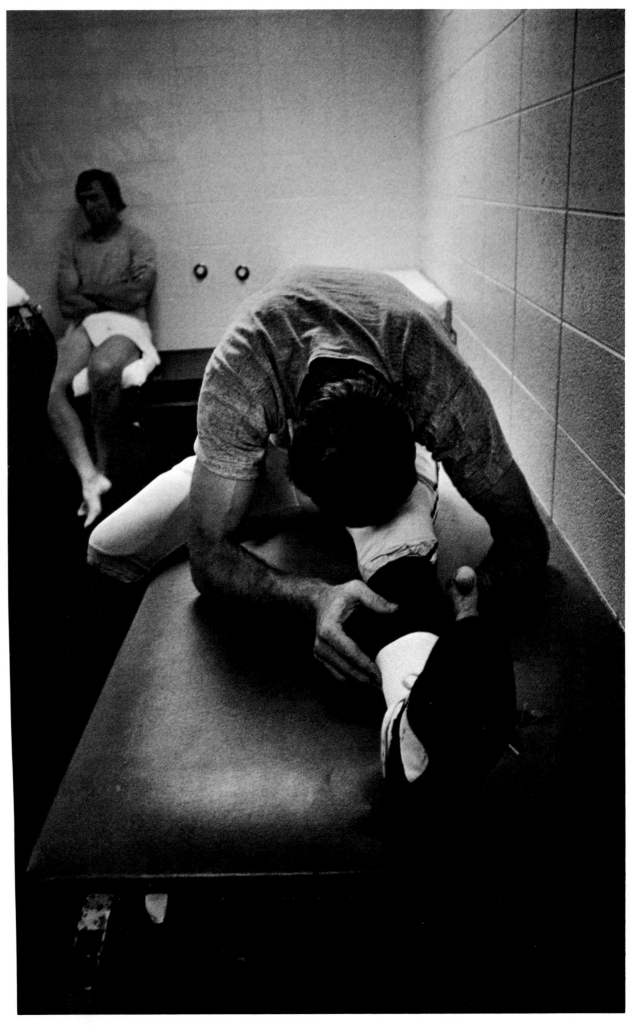

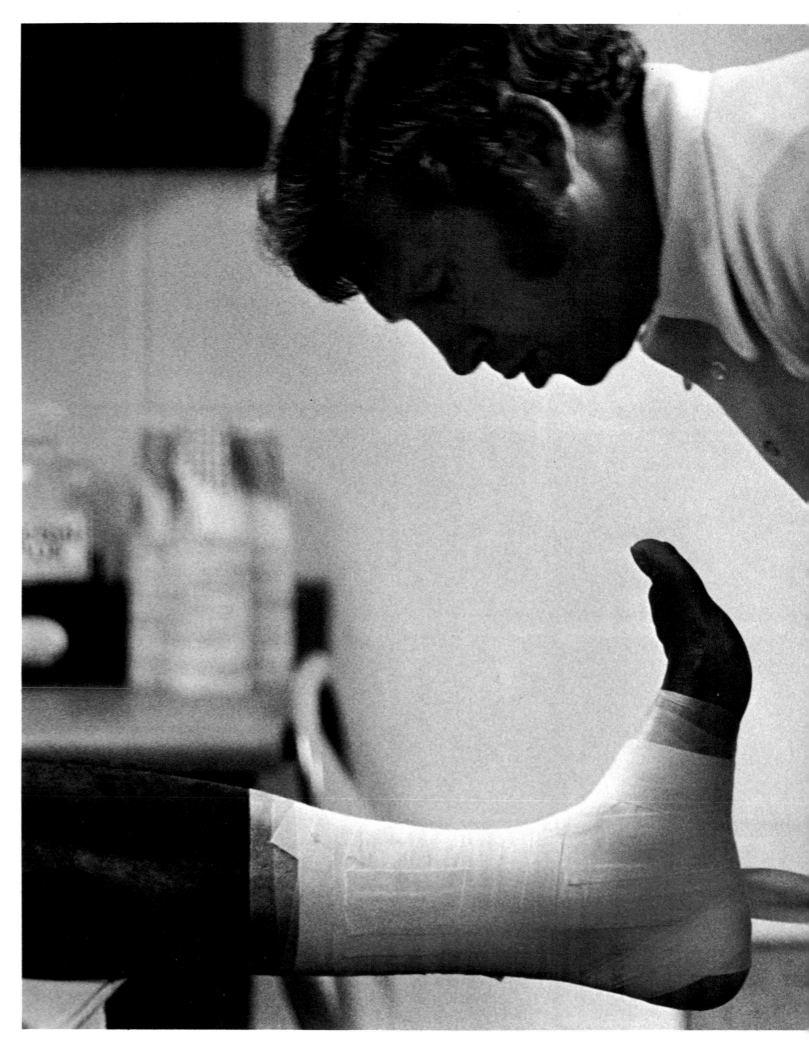

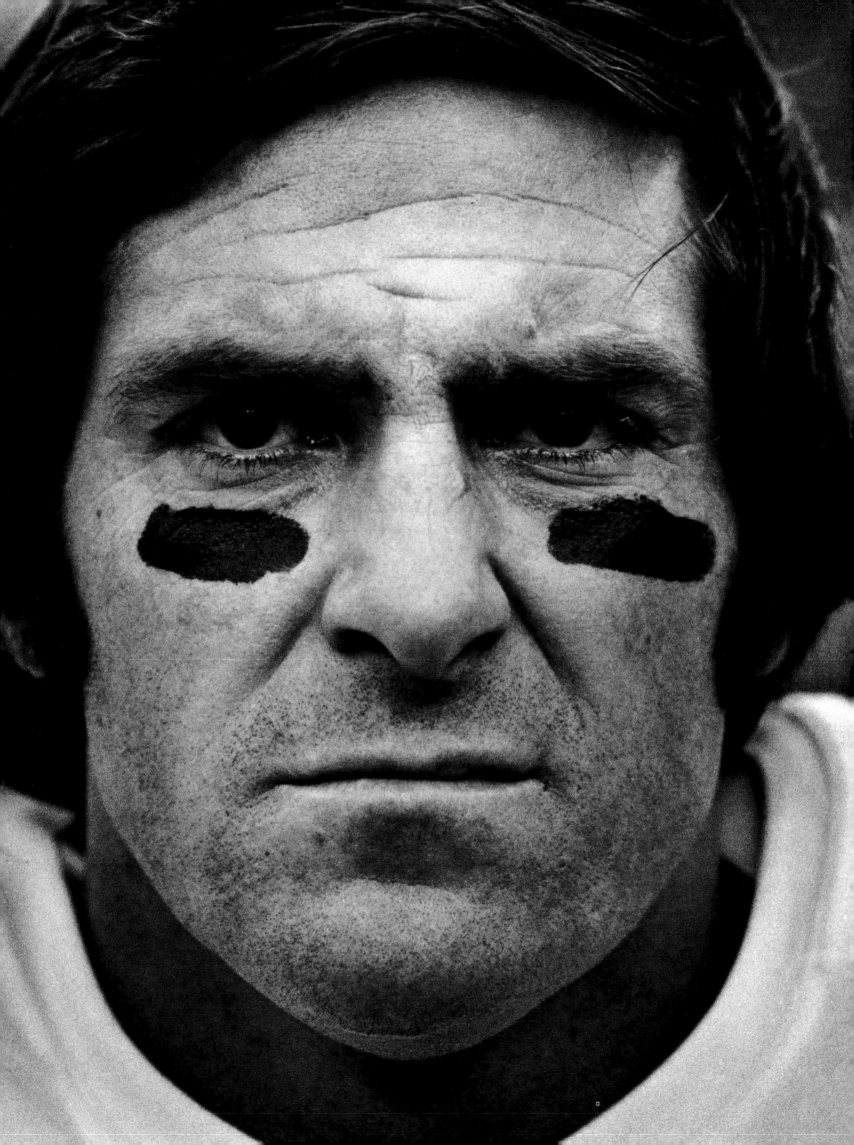

The Fire Is Here

Prologue

The editors of this book wanted me to say something fresh, something incredibly new, something amazingly forceful and surprising about football.

How do you *do* that?

How do you find a way to say new things about such a familiar subject?

I looked at a few hundred exceptional photographs.

Nothing happened.

I went to a few football games.

Nothing happened.

Nothing except the old miracles, the old and dearly similar rushes and cries and amiable brutalities.

But even those, I saw, were not as brutal, close up, as I had imagined they might be. I had somewhat dimly hoped for bonecrushing, rib-destroying, skull-crunching truths delivered in avalanches around, about, over, and on me.

The harder I looked the less I knew. The more I searched the less I found. Gazing around at the running teams, the crowd, the blue sky, I thought, come on, God, give me a day like the day when I was ten years old and discovered I was *alive* for the first time.

Don't give me facts; give me Revelations. Hit me with a bolt.

Nothing happened.

Except, suddenly, something *did* happen.

On a particular Saturday in November, 1974 I stumbled into the Los Angeles Coliseum to see some college teams play football.

All the lightning and fever and pandemonium in history flattened me.

Because what I saw was the Notre Dame-USC game.

Remember that one?

During the first half I drank beer to console myself, since USC was losing its soul, heart, guts, and shoes out there in a dreadful weather of loss.

During the second half I drank beer to celebrate.

It was all magical, of course. I *made* it happen. At the kickoff for the second half I prayed:

Run it all the way for a touchdown.

Which is exactly what happened.

The people, on their feet, raved and screamed and yelled for the next hour.

Because USC just kept running that ball and totaling out the Irish. The people never once stopped shouting and shrieking. When all the yells stopped and we dragged ourselves out laughing and staggering, my daughter, whose first game this was, turned and said:

"Is it *always* like this?"

"If you're lucky, once every ten years!" I replied, laughing wildly. And we blundered happily off among all the delirious, feverish, similarly blundering people who had been sitting in electric chairs for the last 90 minutes with a billion volts full on, charging and recharging their dynamos. Everywhere you looked were sunburst faces, eyes exploding with fire, mouths wreathed in Greek comedy smiles. With, of course, a few Notre Dame losers lurking here or there, dodging the crowds, shadowing themselves away to their cars to unearth triple martinis or quadruple scotches.

I warmed my hands at the passing throng. I warmed my face at their faces. I warmed my soul at the sunfires that absolutely blazed in their flesh as they went away in the autumn afternoon.

We are sun worshippers, I thought, and this has been a day of fire and light and joy and such dazzling energy as shucks the years and puts on youth like a bright suit.

I was reminded of this again a few nights later. Still not knowing what I would write in this Prologue, I was in a book store when a friend nudged me and we stood talking weathers and sports and elations.

"My God," he said at last, "wouldn't it be wonderful if medics could plug in on the energy that jumps out of a crowd at the Coliseum?"

"Hey, yeah!" I said, waiting.

"Compact all that energy in a machine and shoot that juice into all the cancer victims in the world and—"

"Cure them?" I supplied.

"Cure them clean through and through!"

"What an idea!" said I. "That's it, by God, that's it! The thing I've been searching for. Eureka! It's found!"

And I wandered off imagining a machine that made a conduit to channel the lava fires, the crowd-electricities, the mob-energies to be delivered into hospital rooms to raise Lazarus, and into old folks' homes to tap-dance the palsied feet and rear up the fragile white-moth people into incredible dances.

What a world that would be!

Will we ever do it, treat the football stadium and its running buffalo tribes on the field and its surging pulses of men and women in the stands as Numero Uno energy-producing field hospitals for the dead to be raised and the sick to be cured?

We've only begun to think of it.

Sport might one day soon teach us so much about energy and spirit as will revitalize the whole area of medicine, psychic medicine, geriatrics, and micro-biology. One really grand game of football might be enough to kick over 10 trillion bubonic germs, send the rats and their fleas back to the seaports, and evict the graveyard tenants forever.

One could easily imagine teams in 2001 playing under such names as the Lazarus 11, the Resurrection Reds, the Easter Morning Whites, or the Ascensionists.

The American Medical Association would tabulate the teams, and the Bureau of Power and Light would lay the cables and transmit the impulses. Football fields would become vast hearthing places where the burning of happy souls would be broadcast by new equipment to the nearest emergency hospital or children's ward. Cables might be run out along the Pacific deeps to the nearest lepers' colony and for the first time in 10,000 years the people with the look of the lion, the lost souls on abandoned isles, might be shaken to health, flaked of their illness, washed in the blood of the lambs and colts, which of course are names for other teams in any years, and caused to swim home singing the praise of pigskins to form new churches. Said churches having coaches for ministers, priests, and — pigskin aside — rabbis, where confession might be admitting you don't like hockey, so Lord forgive me, and baseball? That's not so hot, either. A church, affiliated with a hospital, where Mary is on one side in a chapel, Knute Rockne on the other, and Christ, in between, wears a helmet and does not despair.

All pretty wild? Yes, no, maybe.

I remember the fire, I remember the warmth. I remember the joy. I remember the hearthing place of that game with 100,000 Jehovah's Witnesses, whether they knew they wore the label or not.

You've all been to similar games and come out dressed in coats of many colors, made up of a thousand invisible lights and shared moments.

Which is the long way around to finally telling you what in hell I'm doing up front here in this book. I was concerned about taking the assignment because I was afraid of repeating threadbare cliches.

But in accepting this task, I remembered going to Houston eight years ago to meet all the astronauts and move around in the training areas where the Apollo missions prepared for their moon flights. I saw everything. I saw too much. I telephoned *LIFE* and asked them to fire me. No, sir, they said. We believe in you.

How much time do I have? I asked.

Twenty-four hours, they said.

I woke the next morning with the handle I needed to fit the astronauts and their jobs: I was looking at a theatre of history where men *rehearsed* history in the same minute detail as actors, directors, script-writers, on simulation-stages, in order to run out to the moon and make time and history real.

I finished my article for *LIFE* in five hours.

The metaphor, the lightning, had struck me.

And now here, on the green field, asking, the lightning has struck again and the answer, the concept, the idea is: ENERGY.

What you have in this book is a collection of photographs of energy frozen for a moment so you can look at it, enjoy it, warm your hands in recollection, warm your hearts with remembrance. The fire is here. The wild blood is here. The joy is here. The freedom is here for you to touch, turn, and rekindle.

Will the Lazarus teams one day a century from now play at eternal scrimmages and total up grand points not only on the lit board but in the tubercular sanitariums and cancer encampments of the world? Who can say? Who would dare predict? Who knows? We know so little of the miracle of stuffs that we humans are. The mystery of our blood and fire and energy is just that: still a mystery after 10,000 years of religion, and a few hundred of truly operative medicine. We have sunlight, and atomic energy, and the tumults and shoutings of fire in football crowds to examine and put on like gear, to run in like founts.

Maybe somewhere along the yardages from one goal to another, we may just catch immortality, turn into a mob of sunflowers looking up at that passing symbol of freedom and elation, that football that drifts forever, and may never come down.

Worth thinking about, anyway. Worth trying to figure an AC-DC plug that might fit and run the wires from stadium to sickroom and tune the Life Force in after the evening news on Channel 5.

If the fire fits, put it on. If the energy suits, wear it like a glove. If the joy is just the right size, tilt it on your head. If the sun at noon and a football at four on a late autumn day look much the same, reach up, grab, carry. Run for your life, laughing. Pursued not by fates and furies but by outrageous laughters and incredible delights.

Here's the book. Here are the photographs of men on their way to becoming fire, burning their images in chemistries on papers in darkrooms to be leafed in later years.

Aren't you glad I waited in the middle of the field for something to touch me?

Aren't you glad that I was lucky and something did at last touch and burn and change?

What a relief to know what I now know about football.

The shadow races on the grass. The ball drifts like an eternal balloon in a sky that is always sunrise.

If you don't mind, I'll just run out after the long toss. Years from now, I may even catch it.

Ray Bradbury

Los Angeles, California

April 24, 1975

From the Instincts Up

Part One

Pro football is excessive. It's all out of proportion, beyond bounds.

It's an orgy of violence; an obsession with superiority; an excess of commitment, effort, and discipline; a wallowing in flesh and will.

Pro football demands too much of too many people. It magnifies and focuses the gut drives and the instinctual cunning; it pours a boiling mix of massive bodies and roaring psyches onto the floors of Sunday's arenas, and shakes society's consciousness with the primal energy of masculine confrontation.

Pro football is excessive.

Pro football is a game of passion.

The two go together; excess and passion. Passion doesn't come in small boxes, with tissue paper and ribbons. Passion comes only in whirlwinds and floods. It inundates and uproots; it takes the normal experience of life and breaks it free of usual boundaries. It begins deep within, feeding on the energy of instinctual animal needs and then expands outward through all the layers of the human personality—through ego, intellect, emotion, and creativity. To reach its height, it demands a focusing of attention, a dedication amounting to crusade. To find its outlet requires a challenge, a goad, a partner-opponent. And when it's all just right, when every engine is switched on at once, it doesn't matter who is involved or how they got there, everyone blasting loose together.

And this is the nature of football. It takes the raw ego power of personal combat and refracts it through the intricacy of intellect and the grace of physical brilliance. It is a consuming crusade, an ultimate challenge; it takes whatever personalities venture onto the field and pulls them past themselves.

The basis of football is physical force applied in the rudest way, encouraged by rules that envision full-speed collisions as normal events. This is the basis of the passion of the game. A man plays football from his guts out, from his instincts up. His identity, his ego is under the fundamental attack that comes from the threat of physical dominance. This is what linemen, in particular, think about on the sidelines, their eyes hard under hard hats; they think about the past and future battles that build the structure of the game.

These crashing combats are a brutal test for the most fragile part of a man's psychology: his self-image and his self-respect. The challenge is so obvious, so blatant, so sweaty and fleshy, so intimately and intensely invasionary. A cry, a collision and a man can be down on his back, muscled over, trampled, beaten, fallen on, and rolled over, with foreign smells, and foreign arms, and foreign will dominating his body and mind.

It's an overpowering experience and it connects deeply into the primal instincts, back to the old tribal customs of rule by physical dominance, back beyond that to the mating battles of animals, the physical testing of worth to the species. No matter how secure a man is, how well-adjusted and mature he is, when he puts himself in the way of this intimate, physical confrontation, he surrenders some part of himself to these archaic drives, and he releases an energy of survival normally capped securely by social conventions.

And so the big men of the sport stand and stare out at the field; they stride up and down the sidelines; they sit on the bench hunched over elbows on knees, great taped hands working and twisting; they wait for the battles to come that they can't always win, but want never to lose.

Violence is the base note of the sport, the context of the action. But sheer mayhem is not the nature of the game's attraction. Mindless, random physical combat would be, at the least, a stupefying bore.

The point to football is that it is a game built from violence upward into a structure of great, layered delicacy. Energy boils off the shattering collisions in steaming clouds, and is then put to the service of skill and intellect.

A leading voice, as befits man's status as the thinking animal, is at the level of mind. One definition of humiliation is the great, dumb giant outwitted by the clever hero; superiority in human terms is superiority of intellect; and thus it's important that football is not only the most persistently violent of all

team sports, but also the most structured, detailed, and precise. The more intelligent team wins in football almost invariably, and the great coaches and players apply themselves to the finely granulated complexity of their game with the passionate intensity of poets and physicists. The two most important pieces of equipment for any pro team are the football and a computer.

But even though the complexity of the sport is an endless study—nuance of technique, creativity of play design, overall scope of strategic concept—this mental aspect of the sport can never escape its roots in combat. Football does not alternate between violence and precision; it is both, together, continuously. In fact the precision depends on, is *built* of, the violence. Coaches spend lifetimes constructing detailed diagrams, prescribing exact angles and clear stopping points. When these diagrams are translated into bodies on the field, they can only operate with collisions as their inevitable conclusion. If a tackle is to be trapped right *here;* if a linebacker is to be cracked right *there;* if scant inches of empty space are to be created at all, then people must be stopped exactly where the plans say. The force has to come from mass times momentum, the clarity of effect from full-speed collision. The intellect is brought to life through the passion of personal battles.

A clash of wills, drawing on both strength and intellect, and then, like the sun sparkling on a turbulent wave, the brilliant talents of the ball players jump out against the heaving background. Even the bulky linemen jitter and gyrate with the balance of dancers, and the people in the "skill positions" put on a mind-boggling show of cutting, leaping, full-bodied, finger-tip dexterity.

It is finally here, in the dramatic tension between hammering violence and spectacular grace, that pro football attains its impelling force. It's one thing to execute skillful maneuvers on an empty stage or a practice field, but quite another to produce wondrous feats in the presence of inevitable, devastating physical punishment.

Courage matters; it makes a difference. Football players need an order of courage all their own. Unlike athletes in other hazardous endeavors—such as auto racers and trapeze artists—who often cannot afford even one accident per career, football players are wiped out every week. Violence is not a haunting possibility, it's a continuous, painful reality. The quarterback flips a perfect pass under devastating assault; a runner withstands four quarters of punishment to break off the winning run in the final minutes. It is exuberant defiance of intimidation, brash beauty thrown in the face of grinding brutality. It is the passionate assertion, "I am!"

The game is a multi-leveled challenge, and one that each player must meet at every level. The heart of football involves no secondhand confrontations through indirect means such as bats or baskets or nets. With the exception of the field goal, which has been fittingly devalued in recent seasons, the entire game of football is embodied in the men who play it. The players themselves are the implements and the obstacles. If a team wants to attack the opposition at some point, it has to attack the *man* at that point; and attacking him, it has to contend with all of him — not just his eye-hand coordination or his mental alertness but all of him: his bulk, strength, skills, courage, concentration, intelligence, endurance, and will.

The demands are excessive, and so is the response, and that's why *A Game of Passion* is more than a metaphor. Professional football players are alive weekly in a world of rare energy and power. It's a world that demands intensity, involvement, and heightened awareness of the smallest details in an avalanche of experience. The feeling can't be controlled; it's a sensory overload, an emotional slalom that can only be ridden to its inevitable end. And there is little life can offer to match the exaltation, the sky ride, that comes with thrusting through the dense bombardment on the field, through the manic energy gusting down from the stands, and into the electric glory of triumph.

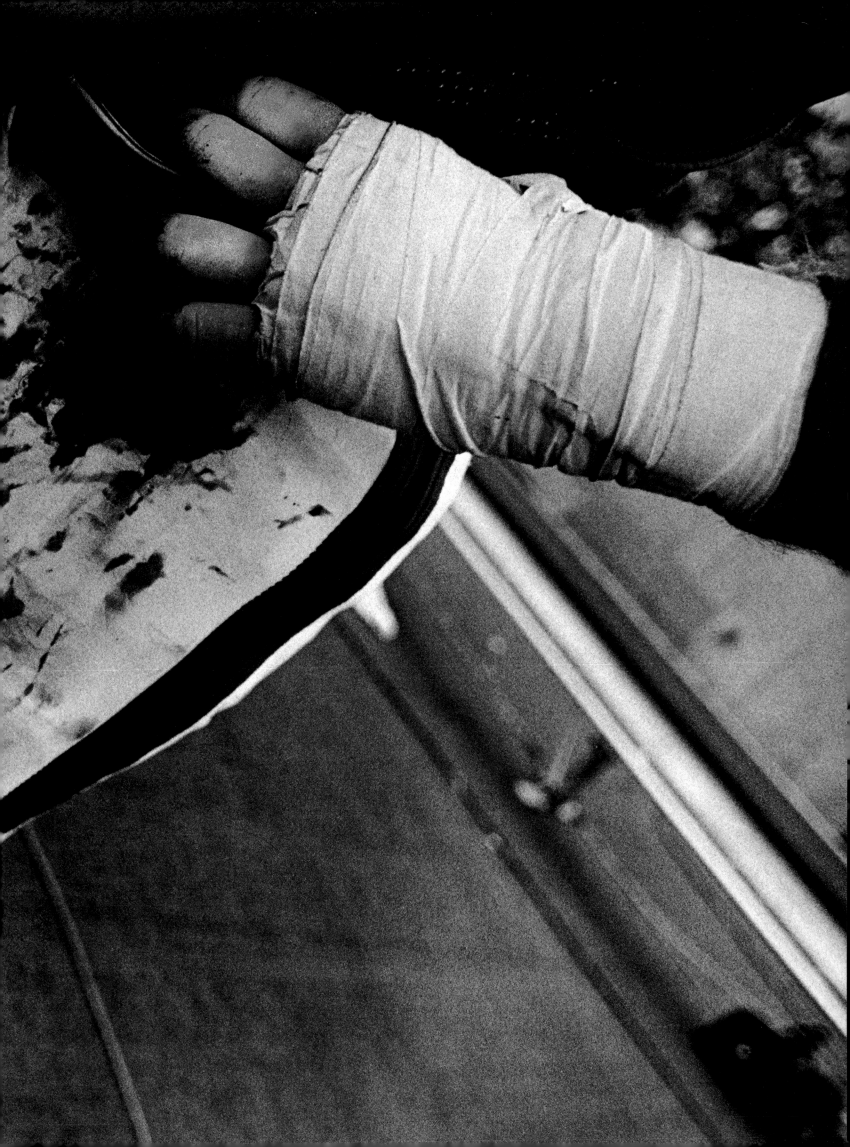

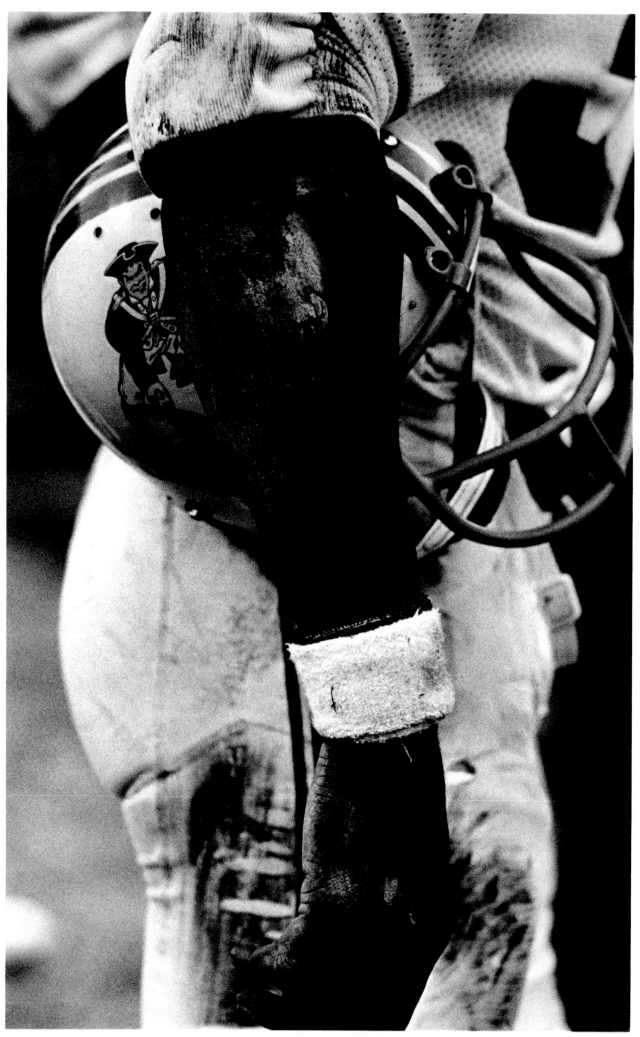

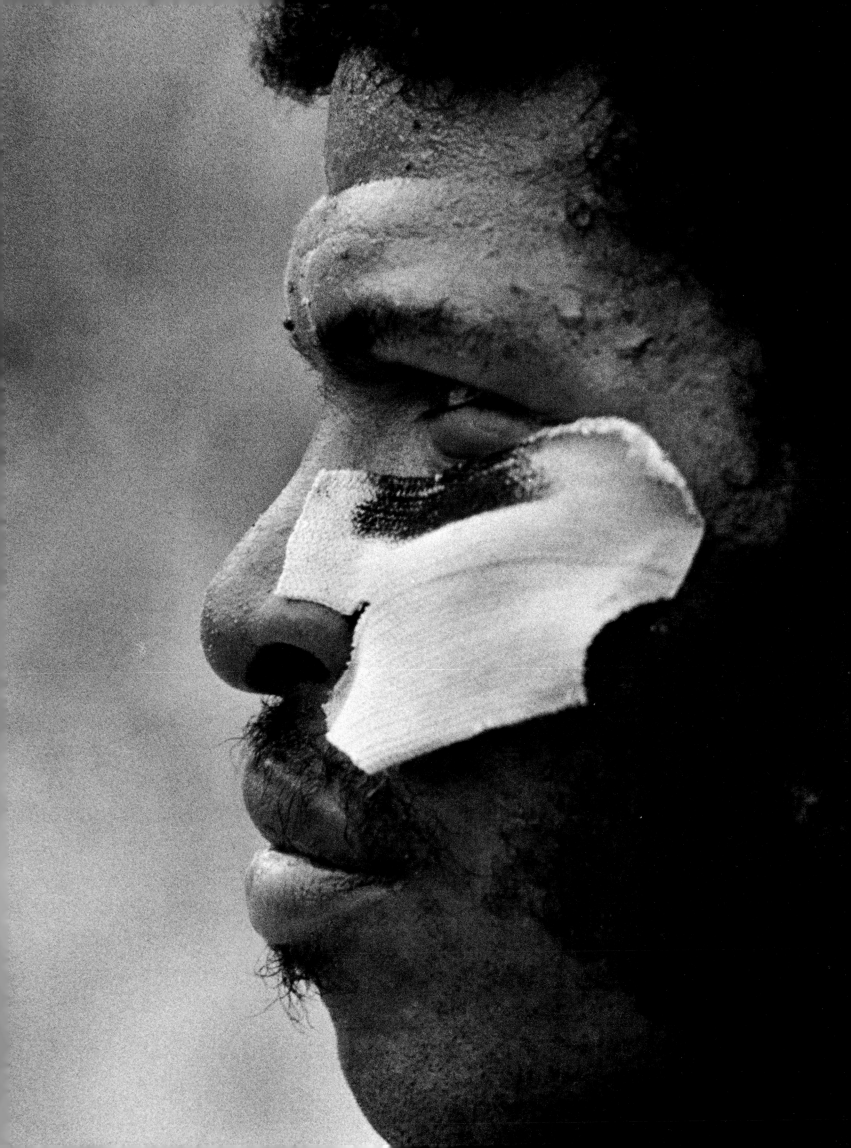

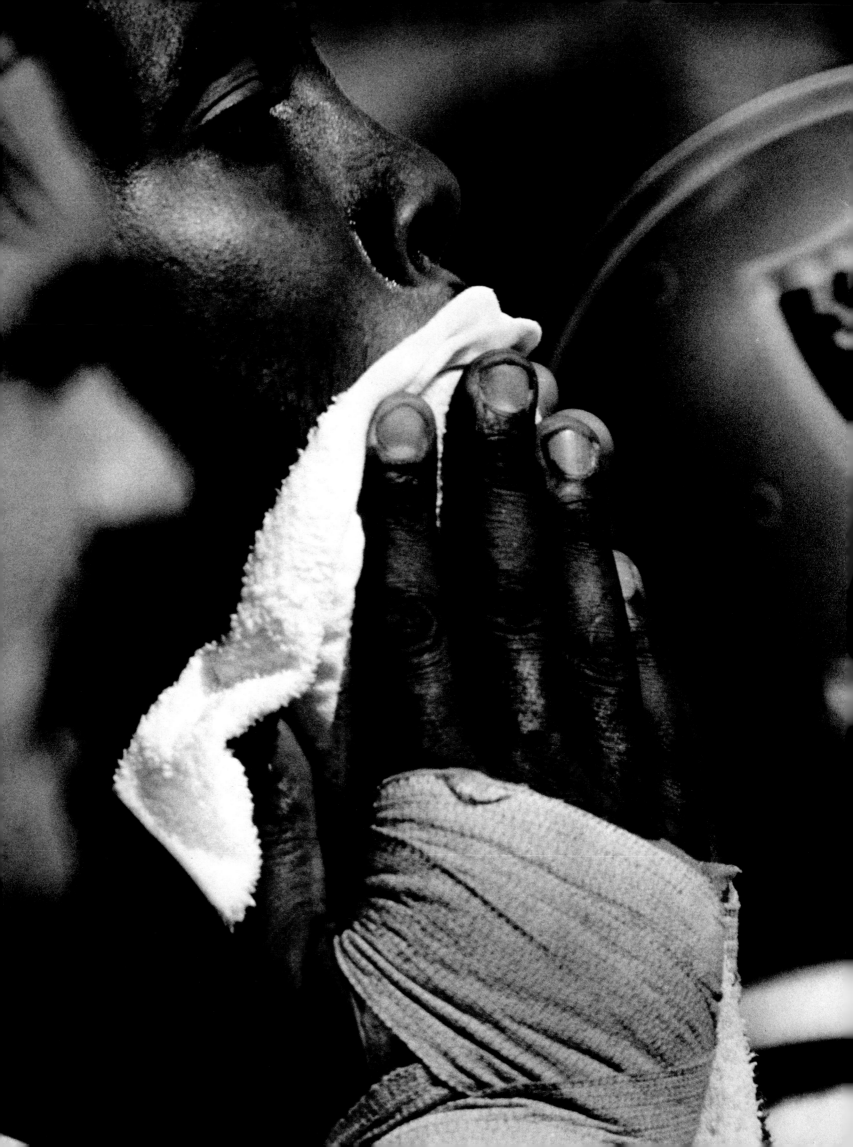

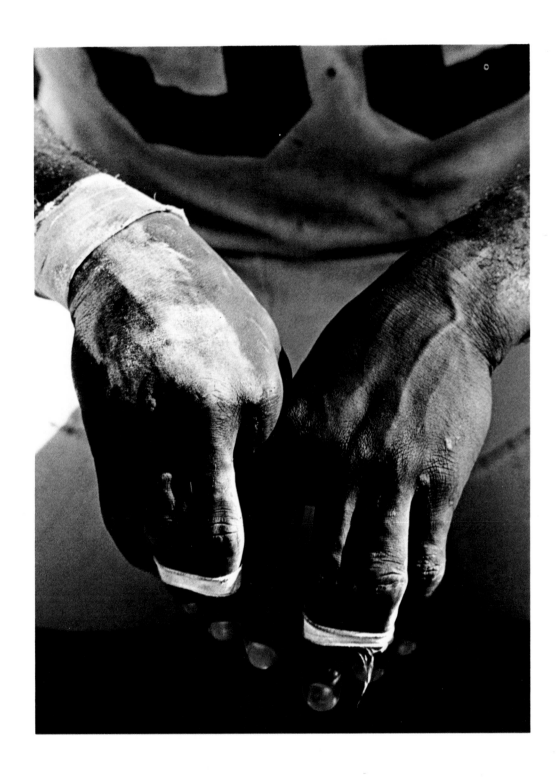

Battles Without Bullets

Part Two

Pro football is a crusade. Success in the sport, even self-respect, demands an intense commitment. It's only a game, a dalliance, a frill in the public life of an overstuffed nation, but once men choose to go out on the field, there is no place to hide. Survival depends on discipline and loyalty, a common crusade begun long before the opening whistle, with each man contributing his mind and body and primal energies to the combustible mixture that is injected into the passions of game day.

It must come this way — an all-out effort sustained overtime, built with care and sacrifice, a joint investment of desire and ego — to sustain a level of passionate involvement once a week. Passion may be uncontrolled, but it is never casual. It breaks boundaries, but it must be directed; it must have a focus. It's not enough that energies come from deep within us. Passion demands an involvement of our consciousness, a deliberate desire to free those deepest forces and feel them as they rush through our systems.

Football is like this. Joining a team is almost like enlisting for a holy war.

In this thought, however, "almost" is a vital word. It's a standard criticism to say that football is *just* like war. Look at the violence, goes this view. Look at the discipline and the suffering and the release of those energies of dominance and destruction that have no place in the context of civilized society.

Look at the fanatics who do some of the coaching, the brutes who do some of the playing.

But likening football to war—even when the comparison is made by football people—misses the point, the whole meaning, to violent passions of football. The physical battle for dominance does pull from one extremity of man's nature; it does call on his most basic needs and drives. But the difference, the difference....

Defensive ends are huge examples of the species, barrel-chested and strong-armed; they swagger and boast and laugh about how many quarterbacks they can eat at one sitting. But it can happen to a defensive end, too. The guard can be coming, and the end's foot can slip as he sets, and the guard can catch him square with the helmet in his gut, and explode him back and down and the back runs free through the hole that shouldn't be there. It can happen, and it's a terrible thing for a strong man to be torn up like that. There's only one saving grace. He may be flattened and bruised; he may be helpless and embarrassed.

But he's not dead.

This is a *game* they're playing. People don't leave their intestines on the ground when they're blocked; they don't lose a leg when they're tackled. The force of collisions in football is often astounding, but it is the lack of resulting damage that is truly surprising. The modern athletes are so well trained, their tolerance for pain so high, their protective equipment so effective, that there is more sound than substance to most of the hitting. Injuries do happen, of course, but coming back from an injury is not quite the same problem as coming back from the dead.

In fact, the way to think about it is not that football is like war. It is that war is like *football*...except for the horrible finality.

Both football and war are thrown up by man's inner turmoil, by his lusts for energy, power, and territorial sovereignty. Both of them feed on the capacity for passionate arousal that is built into man's chemical and neurological makeup. Both of them grow in the hot-house atmosphere provided by clear loyalties and well-defined enemies, by discipline and self-sacrifice, by pageant and pep talks, by flags and drum rolls. War can be confused with football right down to the last moment, and then there are bullets in the air instead of inflated bladders, and an excuse for excitement suddenly turns much too real. Once the fighting starts, only the generals and politicians can afford to think of war as a game.

It's not even accurate to think of war as a natural result of man's animal nature. When animals battle for the rights to sex and territory, they don't fight to kill. They only go far enough to establish where superiority lies and the weaker combatant then concedes and withdraws.

War has to exaggerate these drives, pervert them, make a horror of evolutionary necessity. But football takes these same drives and transmutes them through the creative intelligence of the race. It orchestrates them into a confrontation of mythic proportions, a structure that can support the whole panoply of a society gone to battle. And the results are more satisfying: At most, it's a game; at best, it's an art form.

It's not necessary to turn outside of football to understand its essential passion. Comparisons can be as confusing as enlightening; the danger lies in missing the essential humanness of the experience. Bears can fight, boars can rut; it's not the animal energies that are interesting in themselves, but rather what is done with them. And when nature evolved the human being, it evolved a power transformer.

What each man creates depends on what he is. The same force of creativity filtered through different nervous systems emerges in different ways: as automobile engines and paintings, as plows and books, as pop-top beer cans and the world's tallest buildings.

When the energy is run through the great warrior-dancers of America — where warriors aren't needed in push-button armies and dancing is only for people in tights—it comes out jumping and shouting on the football field. From a place even deeper than the lair of the instinctual drives, comes the need to create, to express, to live into reality the potential that's there inside. Abraham Maslow made a good part of his reputation as a break-through psychologist by observing that for human beings, what is possible becomes what is necessary; talents are needs and potentials are imperatives.

The massive, master athletes who play football are built with combustible possibilities, with power and quickness and courage. Their essence, their being, demands expression. Their nature has evolved the modern game of football.

Their passion for battle, their lust for the sensation of power, can now express itself in a sport that is big enough, violent enough, dense enough, and subtle enough. It's just for the hell of it—and, in the pros, for the money—but it gives those powerful men the chance to experience their rumbling energies at full cry.

Viewed this way, football takes on a certain dignity. It is a way to *play* with passions, to get them all out in relative safety. The game makes it obvious that war is not a natural necessity born in our beastly nature. War is just a failure of imagination, just an intellectual bankruptcy.

In a war-weary century, we can now see that war is a sham.

It's football that's real.

Pro football, then, is a crusade with acceptable consequences. It's aggression without guilt, passion without aftertaste. But it only works when it's taken full-speed, when it's played like it matters until the final gun.

To get themselves ready, pro football players join a new crusade every week. Monday is a day for recovery. Tuesday gets the machinery functioning again. The dedication to game-day excellence begins on Wednesday.

Each game is a new challenge, with new demands astride the familiar structure. There is a new man to face, a new opponent to study in the flickering quiet of the film room, to recall in the lonely hours late at night, to conquer repeatedly in the powerful unreality of the mind's eye. There are new plays to master, a new audible system to pick up, a new technique to develop.

The goal is perfection: zero defects, flawless execution in the coming maelstrom. The week builds through the rhythms of meetings and practice, of thinking and action. If the mind tires or wanders or starts to flap loosely, it must be caught and drilled and honed and focused. If the body tires or falters or wants to slow down, it must be shaken and driven and pushed to new plateaus of strength and purpose.

And as game day approaches, as those 60 minutes of future time pulse larger in today's reality, the entire personality begins to withdraw from the present and step into the coming passions. Friends become objects, families a hindrance. Anything that keeps the mind here and now, instead of then and conquering, is a block to the vital reality. Time is warped by mind, and energy is funneled forward until those 60 minutes are overflowing with intensity jammed into them from the days gone before.

And it is not just the players, not just the people directly involved, who are gearing themselves up for game day. Out in society, millions of other people are also looking forward to game day.

The driving energy of pro football captures a large part of the nation's attention every week in the fall. In the life of modern society, where routine jobs, pre-fab houses, and instant food are the daily reality, any jolt of passion has a powerful fascination. Even secondhand, it's soaked up like water hitting parched ground. Every seven days the nervous system of the whole society — the newspapers, the radio, and especially the television — is saturated with this real-life high and the rush is delivered to every corner of the country.

It's the same for musicians and jugglers, for politicians and football players. At a football game, tens of thousands of fans pour their desires and needs onto the field. And if, individually, they don't have the same investment in the game as the athletes playing, their massed power is enormous. Great waves of passion roll across the field even before the game begins. When the stadium is empty, walking across its floor is unreal. It's like moving across a crater on the moon.

For athletes, game day comes with a slight sizzle, a light crackling washing through the nervous system. The week's production of energy is waiting, and the charge builds slowly, working from the inside out.

While the stands fill in the stadium, the locker room becomes an energy oven as 50 men fill the room with radiations of will and strength, tension and fear. Sometimes it's noisy, shouts and laughs cutting the edge off, letting the valve loose; sometimes it's quiet, the silence rattling with coming battles.

The word comes, the door opens, cleated feet clatter down the tunnel, and the storm breaks out into the light, into the storm roaring down from the stands. It's a force field, a generator with one pole in the players and the other in the people high above, and the players shake off loose energy, jumping and high-stepping and pounding on pads.

There is quiet for a moment, a pause before the blare of a band, and then the stomach seems to crack wide open with the blast of the crowd. Out of the sky comes a high-tumbling ball and big men run full out into pounding, pad-crashing collisions.

The monster is loose.

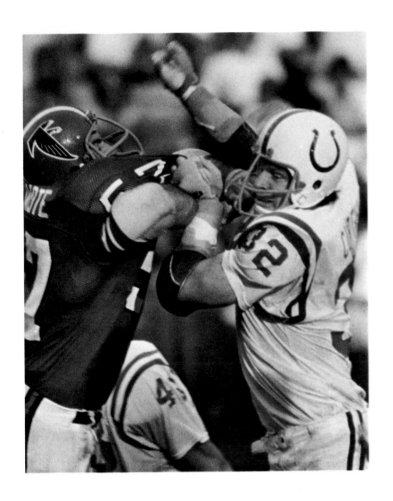

Life in the Crucible

Part Three

Football is people creating passion from intense competition. It is people choosing up sides so there can be clear-cut enemies and obvious focus. It is people agreeing that all-out is all right, that civility can wait awhile, that now it's time for another life.

It's an archetypical confrontation. At any one time in the game, there are two groups on the field: builders and destroyers. The offense tries to construct something useful out of the shattering chaos on defense. The two opposing forces lock together in bitter conflict, yet somehow it seems that the more desperate the competition, the more meaningful the cooperation, and the result is passion in many varieties.

The defensive people first: bigger, usually, swaggering a little, an edge of defiance in their gestures and their cries. They stand only half-bent to their huddles, with legs crossed and hands on hips. They can't take much regimentation; they're a taste too wild for the disciplines of offense. They are rebels, wreckers, specialists in the art of demolition.

Their role is recycling. If a car has died, it can be left on the street to take up space, or it can be attacked and dismantled, smashed into reusable pieces. This is defense. Defensive people destroy the unfit, rip it apart, send it back in shattered pieces for recasting. It is the back half of passion — destruction of the worthless — and it's an operation that breeds a ferocious glee.

The linemen do the first dismantling, pounding and tearing at the offensive innards. These are often the wildest people on the field. Passions barely covered by persona, they quickly break the light leash of their specific assignments and go in crashing, arms flailing, wild for prey.

Behind them are the linebackers, crouched back a little, ducking sideways behind cover. These are more deliberate assassins, their drives more compacted, and they line up their targets like snipers before cracking them backwards.

And behind them, the last line, the deep backs circle and float and swoop in like jet fighters out of the sun. Their fuel is fear. Their passion comes from constant proximity to six-point calamity, and they take out their tension on anybody who's handy.

Three tiers of trouble: It's awesome to see them when they have it together. Watching a good defense is like watching a natural catastrophe in uniform.

Across the line of scrimmage, the offense generates another feeling altogether. They bend precisely into their huddle, hands on knees and feet just so.

Offensive people are builders and carvers, creators of patterns and spaces in a hostile chaos. Offensive players need patience and dedication and endurance and will. Offensive players go to work.

Success for the men of defense brings a savage thrill, but for the offense success is a quieter satisfaction, a workmanlike pride. Passion has been mastered and harnessed to detail, power has served the need of orderly production. The odds are great against the offense, and every successful drive requires as much care as negotiating a mine field.

The offense is built on the linemen, the diggers, the hard-scrabble miners who go down into the pit to hack out cracks in the living wall of defensive animosity, who stave off collapses that can crush the delicate backfield machinery.

Then come the backs, launched by the line into the cross-cutting thresher of the enemy; the backs with their passion beaten into a flinty knot, indomitable pride flinging them into tiny holes as if they were railway tunnels, slamming them into big, braced men as if they were folding chairs, driving them on while armored bodies and focused minds attack their will to continue. Sport puts no harsher challenge anywhere than it does to football's running back. The better he does, the worse it is; the more hits he survives, the more he gets.

The receiver luxuriates in a different kind of space, great expanses of open field where he runs unchecked most of the day, prancing and gliding through the diffuse, shifting zones, drawing a meteor shower of hostile attention only on those rare occasions when the ball arcs out of the scrimmage struggle and transfers the focus of violence to his body. The passion of the receiver bursts out as peacock pride, a vitality that speaks for magnificent talent used too rarely. The receiver is the Mick Jagger of football.

In the middle of it all but strangely alone, the quarterback plays a delicate game all his own. While the field around him seethes with destruction, the quarterback tunes to a finer level. He is the embodiment of the mental aspect of the sport, and the game he plays is one of patterns and flows, of infinite detail and wide scope, a mind game played for control of the subtle energy that orchestrates the gross physical chaos all around him.

It's a game for power on a grand scale, and when the quarterback is master his mind is riding the focused passions of hundreds, of thousands, of millions of people. When he's found the place, he controls the moves of his teammates, the expectations of his opponents, the moods on both sidelines, and the psyches in the stands.

It's a powerful high while it lasts, but it's a fragile thing, an illusory happening, and the greedy outward reach of this unbridled passion can suddenly collapse like a dying star. The quarterback's privilege of living on the mental plane can be leveled by one blocking breakdown—his glass castle shattered by the rude invasions from outside. The seeming power of his thoughts can falter when an injured running back takes their reality to the bench with him. And his whole structure dissolves when the minds on the other team jump one step ahead, when they know him deeper than he can change himself, and they take his strengths and beat him with them.

Even in the good times the quarterback is a man apart, a semicombatant. When times are bad, when the ground seems like quicksand and their air a wall and the offense is smothered into impotence, then the quarterback has to eat the massed passions turned back on himself. He is assailed by the conquering pride of his opponents, the embittered hopes of his teammates, the cheated lusts of angry fans.

But this extreme is illusion, too. The quarterback can perfect things if they are close, but he's not a god. It's the whole game that determines the whole game. Every mind that puts attention on the field has some effect on the outcome. And every man who gets involved has a chance at his own type of passion.

And so the offense gathers its possibilities into the discipline of the huddle. Creation takes forethought: a brief consultation followed by code words bitten off quickly. Then the group breaks toward the defense.

Creation and destruction come mask to mask in a confrontation that begins as a frozen tableau. Powerful action begins with silence, and a football game evolves in this rhythmic pulsing of rest and activity. Each play starts from settled, perfected structures of formation, with heads and necks and backs laid out along sleek lines like rocks smoothed by years of rushing water.

It's a strained quiet, passion bottled under high pressure. And in the silence minds are lively: What are they doing? Why is he there? Do those eyes really see where they seem to be looking?

Thought in shorthand, and then eruption. Time and again, brief moments of explosion rip the quiet, and then die away to be recharged again. And in these cyclic interactions, creators and destroyers evolve the game they want between them.

The obvious level is competition, an all-out battle for supremacy. But the unspoken bond is cooperation, men traveling together to a vibrant world they could not reach by themselves.

The rules allow for 60 minutes of passionate excitement. All that is needed is a good opponent, a foe who demands the full possibility, a fellow seeker for a realm of mad freedom.

Football is people living passion together.

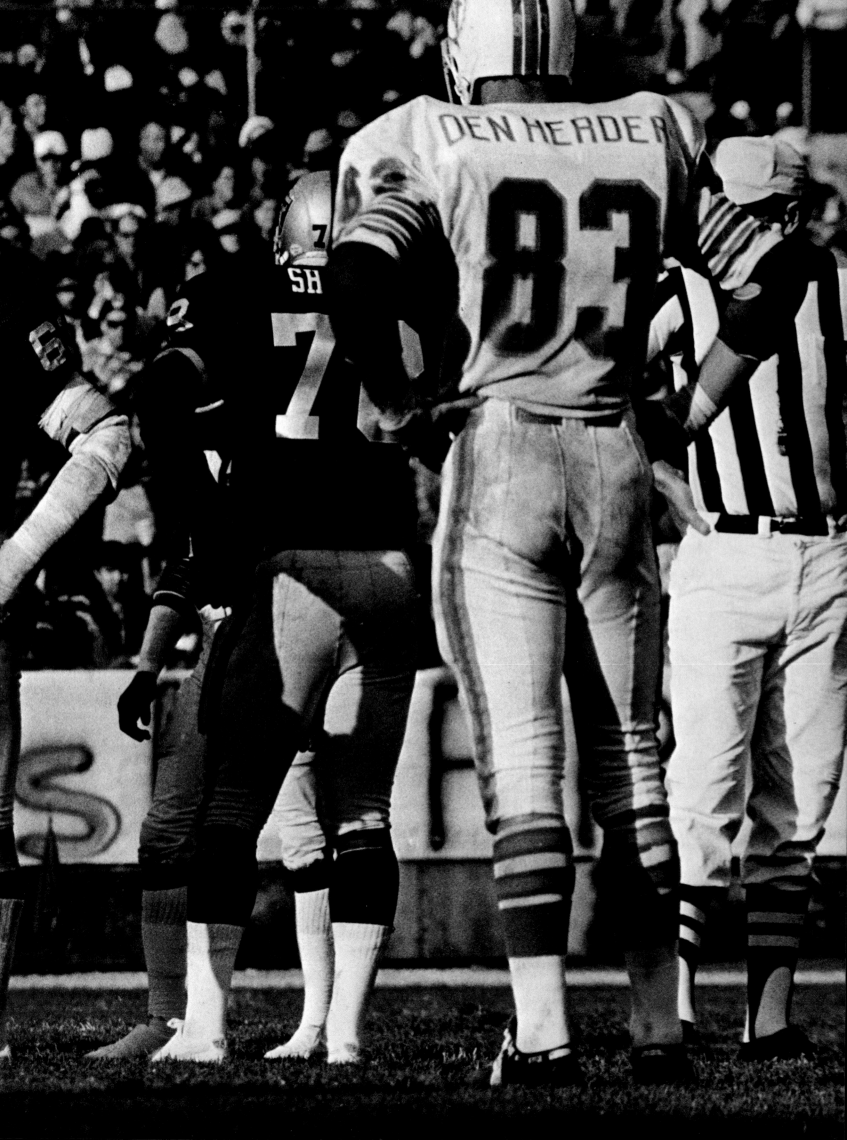

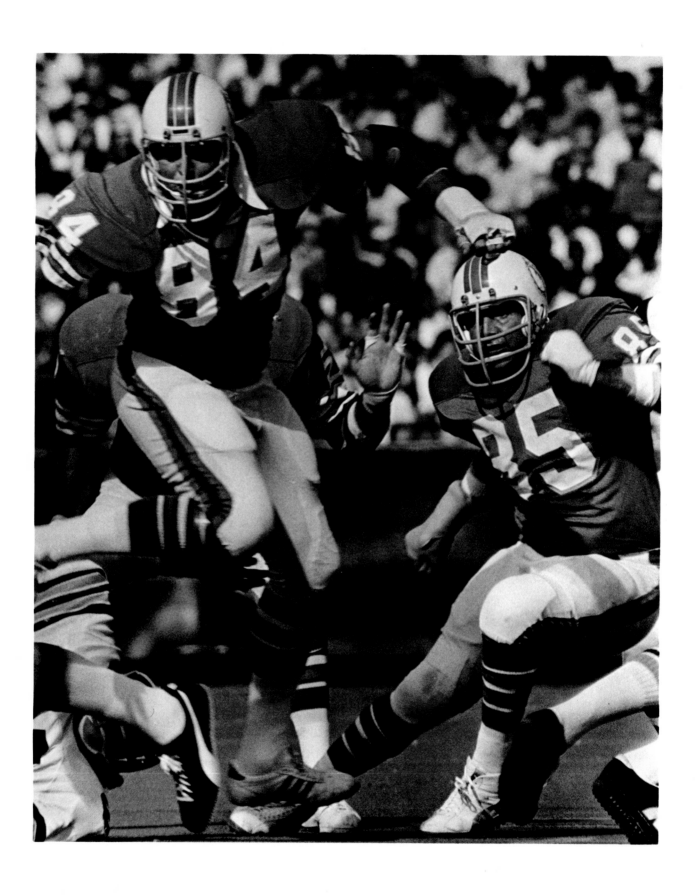

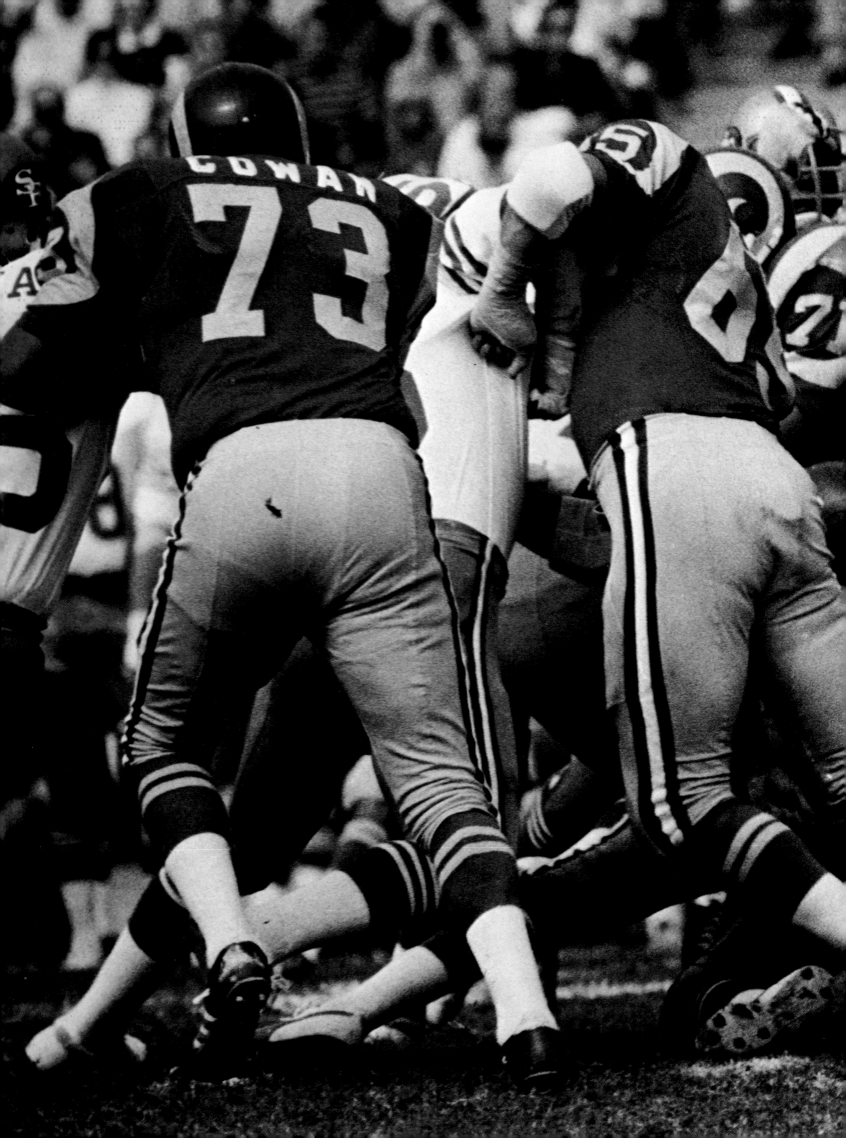

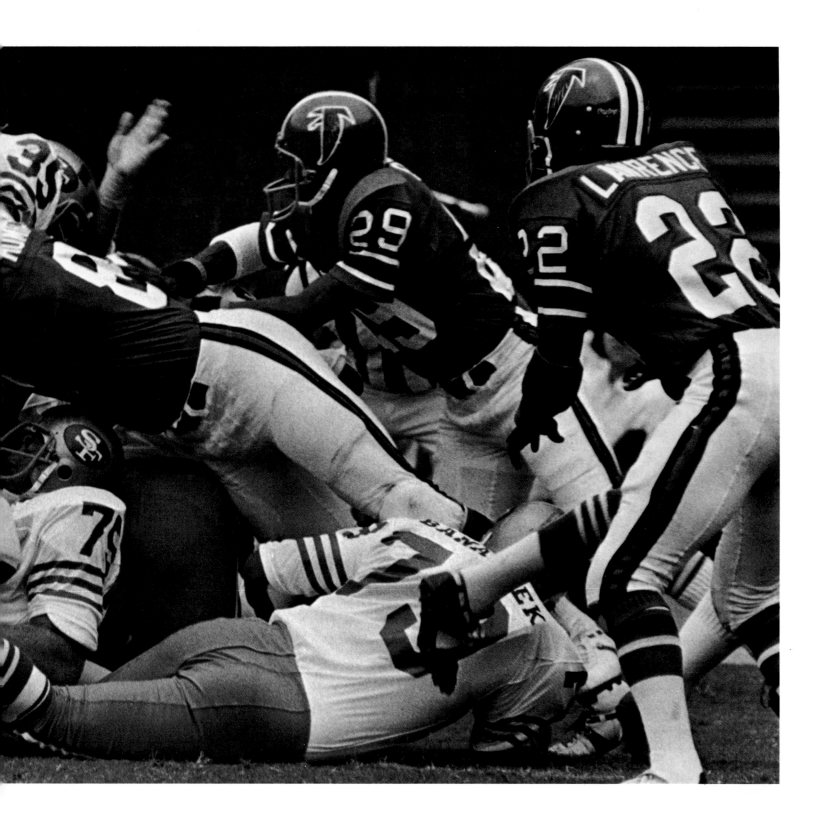

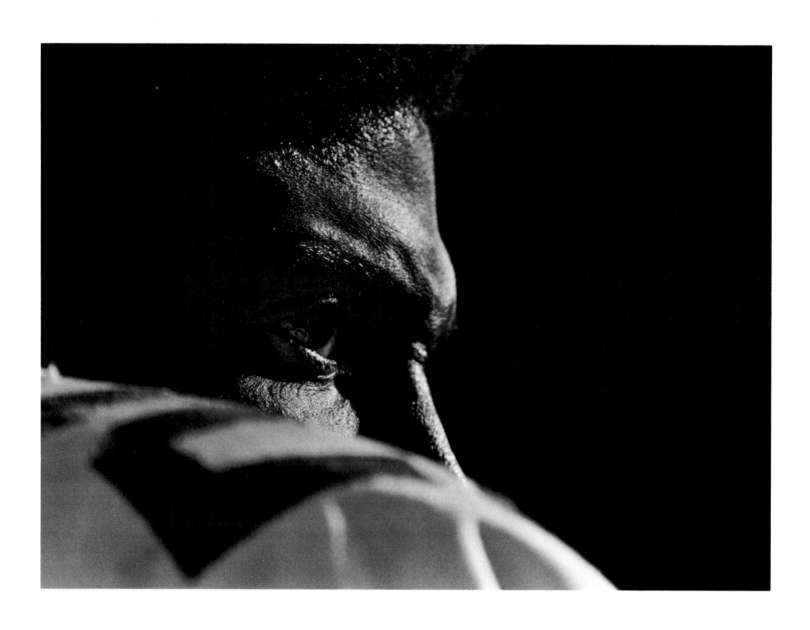

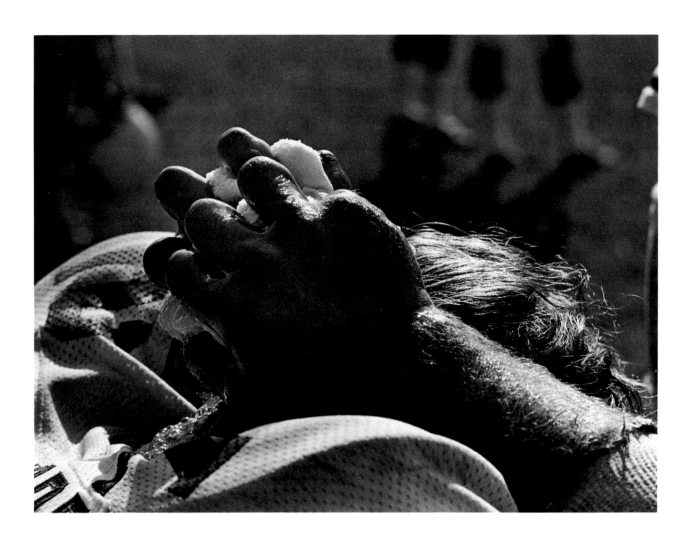

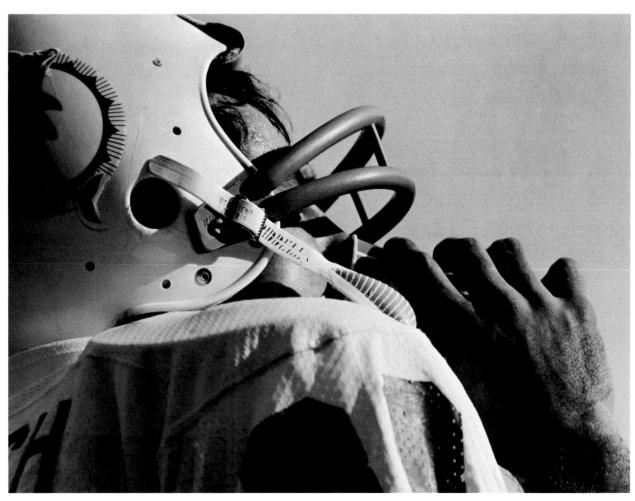

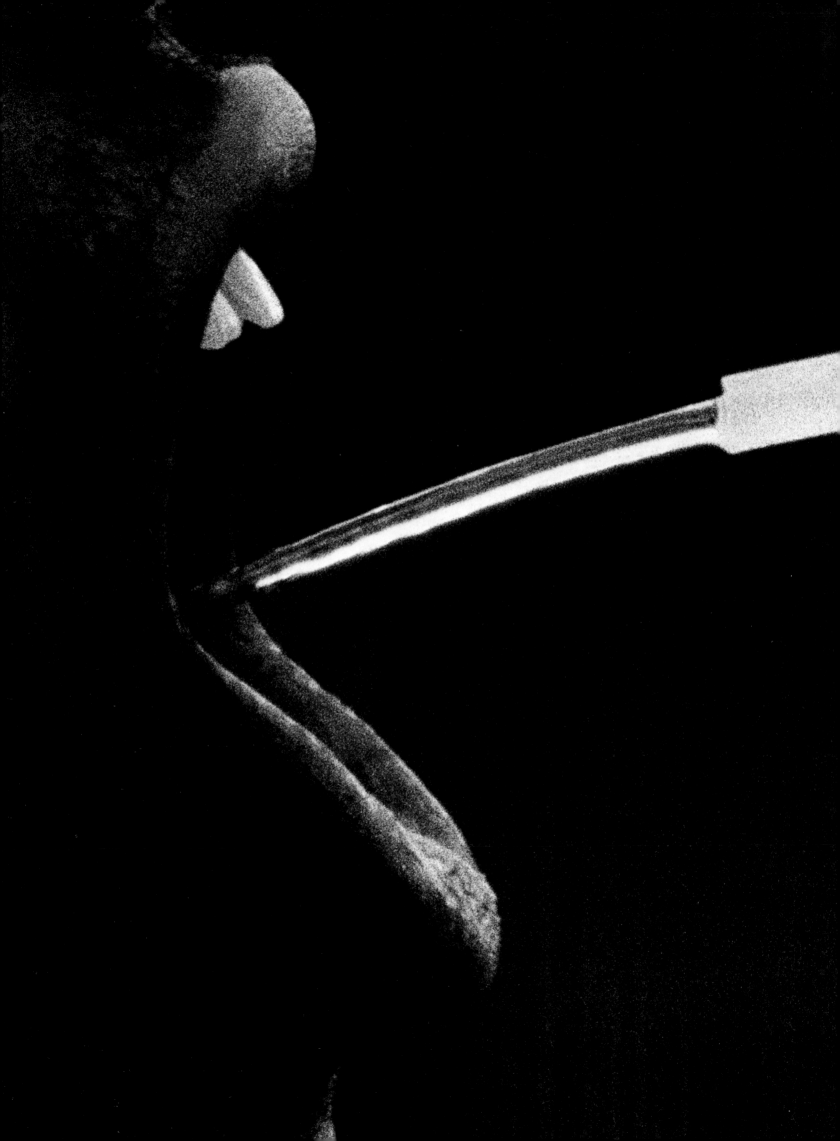

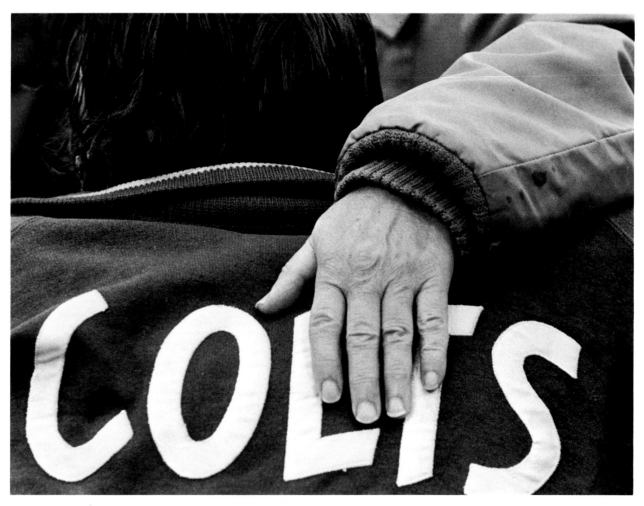

175

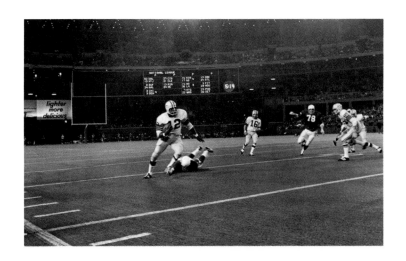

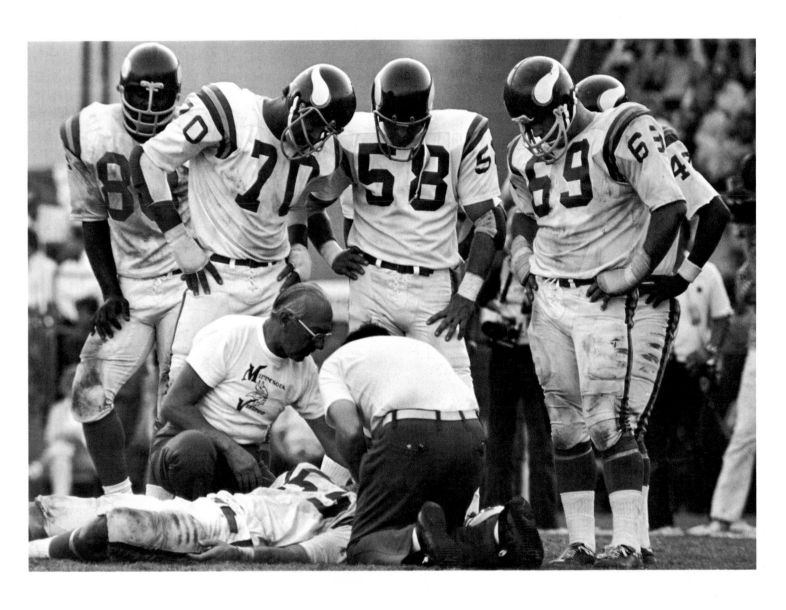

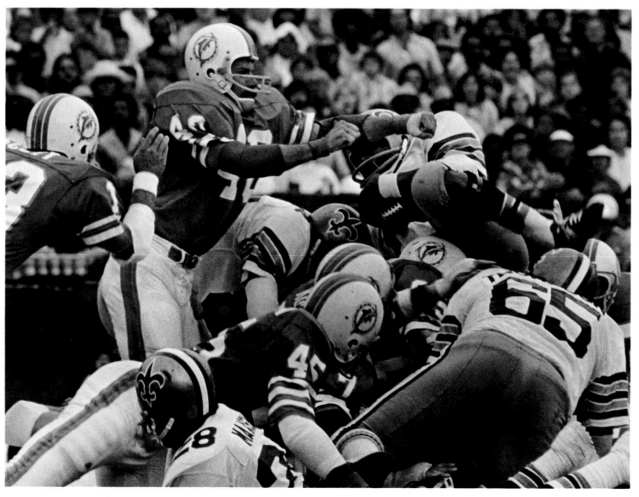

the Realm of Freedom

Part Four

Why do they go through it? What makes a man put up with the effort and discipline, the pain and exhaustion that are such integral parts of this excessive game? If you take pictures of players without their eldritch helmets and padding, if you deflate the heliotropic prose, then it comes down to a simple question: Why do grown men spend their time playing a boy's game?

It's an unfriendly question, of course. It implies that a pro football player has to defend his profession in a way that a lawyer, say, or a fireman needn't bother with. And there's a quick answer available to the game's partisans — too neat, perhaps, but it has a truth. Football isn't a boy's game.

Boys look silly in their lumpy football suits. They go about tackling in an awkward, tentative way dictated by the weakness of their unformed bodies. Children's football is the rough equivalent of little girls clopping around in their mother's high heels.

Football is no childhood hangover, no vapid extension of dodgeball or hide-and-seek. Football is a *man's* game — and successful participation in that first real, pad-cracking scrimmage is the closest thing America has to a masculine rite of initiation.

But that's not the best answer to the question. It's too chauvinistic, too macho. The best answer is another question: Why do most men put up with adulthood?

As a decade of the hip revolution has made clear, most of the roles provided by society for the adult male are not terribly exciting. They usually involve collars that are too tight, and hours that are too long, and possibilities for emotional expression that run the gamut from A to B. For most of us, time passes in familiar patterns of daily routine—Tuesday is pretty much like Friday and life in March is not much different from life in October. It's like eating only the skin of an orange; the sweet juice is missing.

For the men who play pro football, reality is dramatically different. Weeks course through their nervous systems in a powerful rhythm of tension and explosion. Six days build to the peak experience of game day, and hard practices are paid off by immersion in a vortex of intoxicating energy.

The experience belongs to a different world, to a place where being alive has a whole new definition. Football is a game of passion, and the point to passion is that it tears the walls down, rips the rules up, breaks life out of the hedges and fetters that gather inexorably in the gray succession of most daily living.

This is the glory of passion: We are more than we know, and life is richer than we live it. The inside of us wants to get out, is crying to get out, and in the abandon of passion the many layers of our hidden inner nature erupt into our awareness. Passion is an electric leap toward the rest of our birthright.

As a regular punctuation to their normal lives—lives not otherwise exceptional by 1970s standards—pro football players get to plunge into this liberating chaos; and if they can't stay there, if they must come down every Monday to the exhausting reality of supermarkets, stock losses and sore muscles, the periodic high is a powerful addiction. Once a man has found that life can *be* like that, the question is no longer why he does it. The question is how to get him to quit.

True enough, grown men get totally absorbed in this game, forget themselves completely in a world of "X's" and "O's," turn a Sunday pastime into a humorless crusade. Many of them don't even know why, couldn't put it in words if you asked them. They slip from the real to the surreal and back without understanding what they have done.

But if they have no distance, no perspective on their involvement, if they confuse the game they are playing with the life they are living, how are they different from the rest of us?

If people in professional football are sometimes sunk in the intensities of their sport, they can't be separated from school kids aping their peers, businessmen lost in their dealings, housewives soaking up gossip. It's all a natural stage in human development; and it can be said in admiration of football that few games anywhere in society reward the participants so regularly with a walloping bang. At least the passion of the experience justifies the commitment of the energy.

Seen this way, pro football is an experience quite alone, without clear parallels, even in the realm of athletics. Pro football is just another sport only in the sense that rockets to the moon are just another means of transportation. The game has become a world of its own.

And the most compelling thing about it is that football is a game played to get beyond games. Pro football takes much of the abstracted expertise of the overall American "way"—technology, specialization, organization, management theory—and uses these soulless mechanisms to liberate man's elemental passion. It is structure to celebrate freedom, form honoring the formless, the head giving the gut its chance to break free. All routines are traps for the mind and soul, but the routine of football is a trap with a weekly trap door.

Football *is* excessive, beyond bounds. That's why you can't learn much about it by looking at what the participants are like in their daily lives. They are big, powerful men, of course, but past that you can find any type of human being you could want: muscle heads and mathematicians, light show freaks and etymologists, religious leaders, businessmen and ne'er-do-wells. In recent years, the degeneration common to modern society has seemed to eat into the character of players, too. They lead a spoiled life.

But these off-the-field aberrations don't make much difference, because the excesses of football itself make almost anything else seem tame; they are so intense that impurities brought into the game are burned away. Not many of the personalities who come on the field are worthy of hero worship—not many are in any location—but the whole point to the passion of football is that it takes people beyond themselves. Its reality is too harsh for half-efforts. It sucks the players into its validity and shakes them free of at least part of their limitations; it extracts some essence from their deeper layers of self.

The game exists as a thing in itself. It is more than the collection of players. And if it's true that the game is created by the athletes, it's just as true that it makes of the athletes something more than they usually are. To know why men play football, don't look at the men, look at the sport.

It's just a game, of course. It's pointless, of course.

But pointlessness is the point. Energy for the sake of energy; virtuosity for the sake of excitement; passion for the sake of existence; life living its extremes in a glorious, senseless exhibition, like mountains against a sunset.

It's not a sport for everyone. The desire to inflict and sustain full-speed collisions is hardly universal; many people don't even like to watch it happen. But for those who are built to take it, for those who are made to excel in that crucible, football brings a chance to ride life's energies to a peak rarely accessible.

The game's reigning philosopher has summed it up best. Johnny Blood played pro football in the thirties; he was an all-pro on the field, a legend off it. He was an all-time champion at the art of living; he combined careers as a player, coach, traveler, lover, scamp, economist, and myth. The advantage he had over many football players is that he *knew* what he was doing.

And Johnny Blood has summed it up in just a few words.

"The whole point to life," he says, "is to maximize your emotional income."

Feel as much as you can. Jam it all in at once until your head and gut are about to burst. Walk a tightrope in a hurricane while millions watch.

This is power. This is life at another level. If feelings such as these are beyond our understanding, they may sound overblown, excessive, unreal.

They are.

Those who have been there know the truth of this tumultuous sport.

The truth is passion.

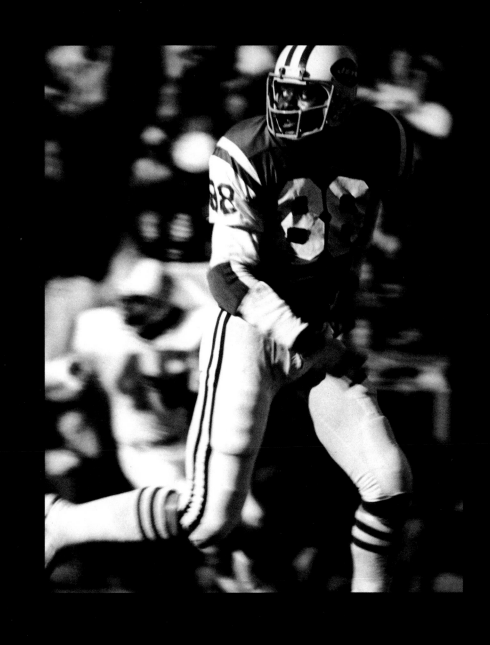

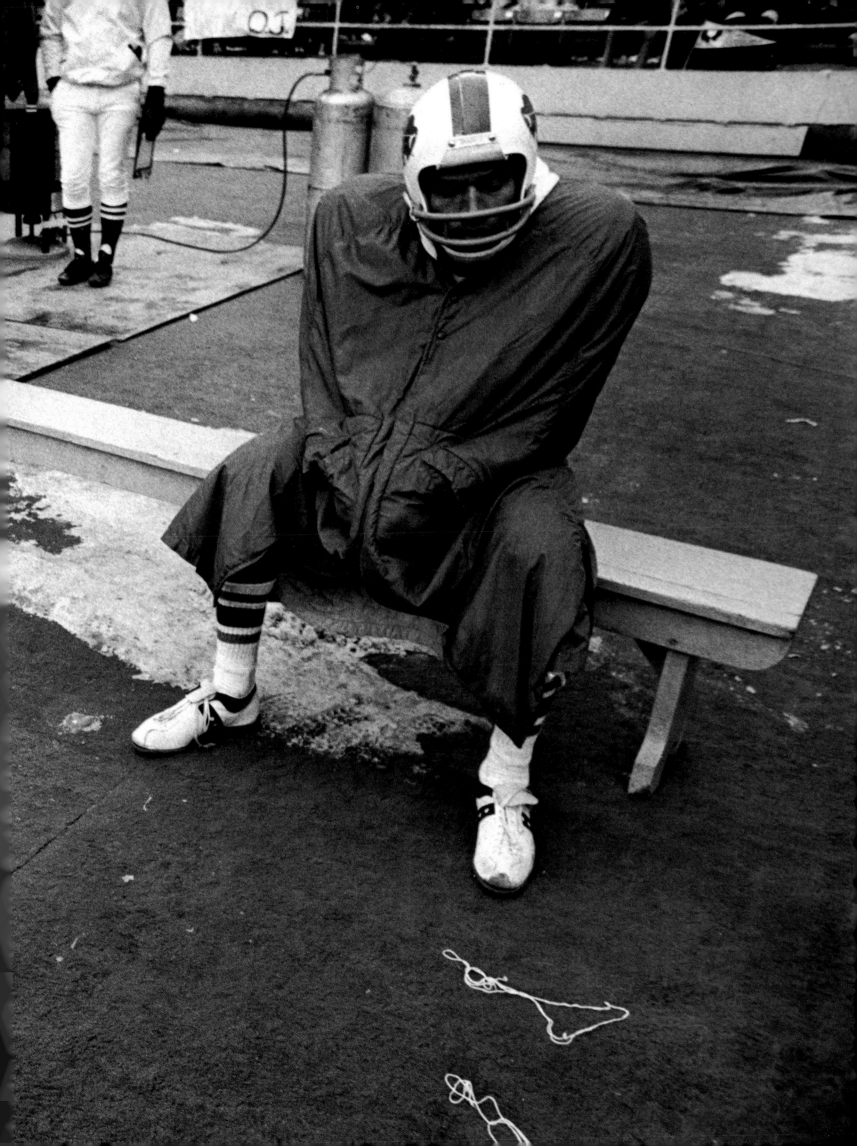

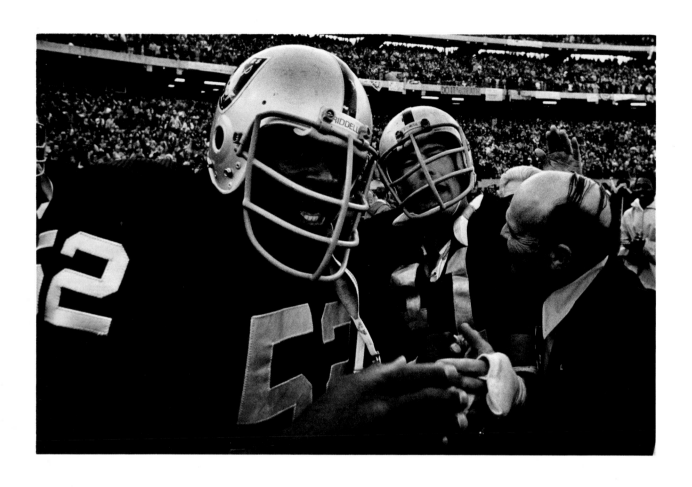

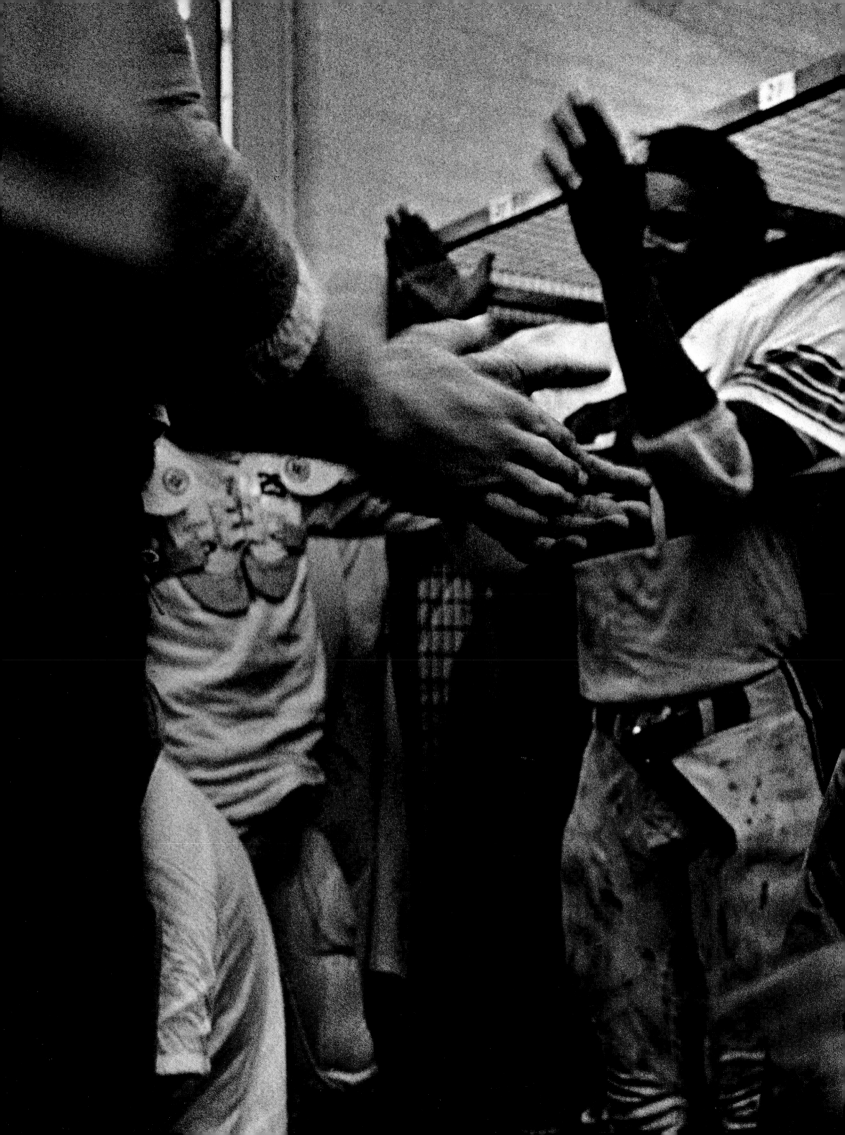

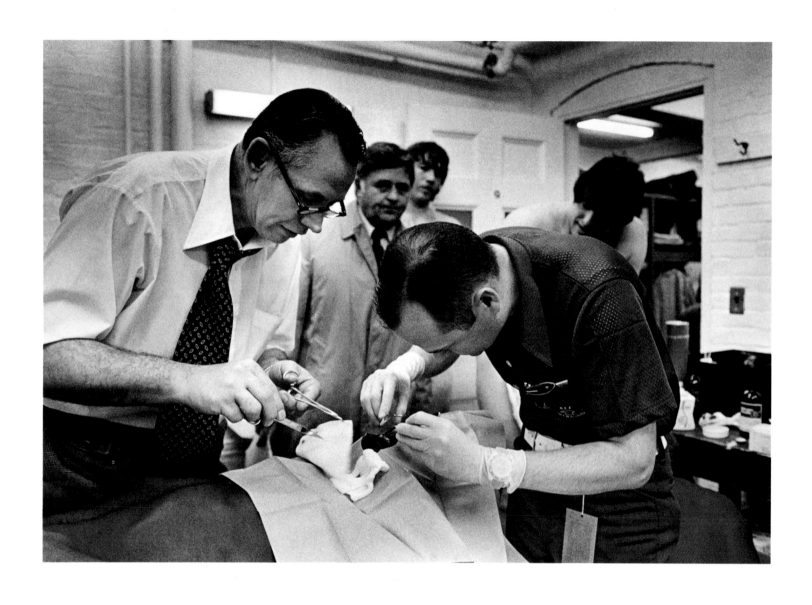

240

All Flesh is One: What Matter Scores?

Epilogue

The thing is this:

We love to see them on the green and growing
field;

There passions yield to weather and a special
time;

There all suspends itself in air,

The missile on its way forever to a goal.

There boys somehow grown up to men are
boys again;

We wrestle in their tumble and their ecstasy,

And there we dare to touch and somehow hold,

Congratulate, or say: Ah, well, next time. Get on!

Our voices lift; the birds all terrified

At sudden pulse of sound, this great and
unseen fount,

Scare like tossed leaves, fly in strewn papers

Up the wind to flagpole tops:

We Celebrate Ourselves!

(Sorry, old Walt.)

We play at life, we dog the vital tracks

Of those who run before and we, all laughing,
make the trek

Across the field, along the lines,

Falling to fuse, rising amused by now-fair,
now-foul

Temper-tantrums, sprint-leaps, handsprings,
recoils,

And brief respites when bodies pile ten high.

All flesh is one: what matter scores?

Or color of the suit

Or if the helmet glints with blue or gold?

All is one bold achievement,

All is fine spring-found-again-in-autumn day

When juices run in antelopes along our blood,

And green our flag, forever green,

Deep colored of the grass, this dye proclaims

Eternities of youngness to the skies

Whose tough winds play our hair and
rearrange our stars

So mysteries abound where most we seek
for answers.

We do confound ourselves.

All this being so, we do make up a Game

And pitch a ball and run to grapple with our
Fates

On common cattle-fields, cow-pasturings,

Where goals are seen and destinies beheld,

And scores summed up so that we truly *know*
a score!

All else is nil; the universal sums

Lie far beyond our reach,

In this mild romp we teach our lambs and colts

Ascensions, swift declines, revolts, wild
victories,

Sad retreats, all compassed in the round

Of one autumnal October afternoon.

Then winds, incensed and sweet with dust of
    leaves
Which, mummified, attest the passing of the
    weather,
Hour, day, and Old Year's tide,
Are fastened, gripped and held all still
For just one moment with the caught ball
    in our hands.
We stand so, frozen on the sill of life
And, young or old, ignore the coming on of night.

All, all is flight!
All loss and apt recovery.
We search the flawless air
And make discovery of projectile tossed—
The center of our being.
This is the only way of seeing;
To run half blind, half in the sad, mad world,
Half out of mind—
The goal line beckons,
And with each yard we pass,
We reckon that we win, by God, we win!
Surely to run, to run and measure this,
This gain of tender grass
Is not a sin to be denied?
All life we've tried and often found contempt
    for us!
So on we hied to lesser gods

Who treat us less as clods and more like men
Who would be kings a little while.
Thus we made up this mile to run.

Beneath a late-on-in-the-afternoon-time sun.
We chalked aside the world's derisions
With our gamebook's rulings and decisions.
So divisions of our own good manufacture
Staked the green a hundred yards, no more,
    no less.
The Universe said, "No"?
We answered, running, "Yes!"
Yes to Ourselves!
Since naught did cipher us
With scoreboards empty,
Strewn with goose-egg zeros
Self-made heroes, then, we kicked that minus,
Wrote in plus!
The gods, magnanimous,
Allowed our score
And noted, passing,
What was less is now, incredibly, more!
Man, then, is the thing
That teaches zeros how to cling together and
    add up!
The cup stood empty?
Well, now, look!
A brimming cup.

No scores are known?

Then look downfield,

There in the twilight sky the numbers run
    and blink

And total up the years;

Our sons this day are grown.

What matter if the board is cleared an hour
    from now

And empty lies the stadium wherein died roars

Instead of men

And goal posts fell in lieu of battlements.

See where the battle turf is splayed

Where panicked herds of warriors sped by,

Half buffalo and half ballet.

Their hoofmarks fill with rain

As thunders close and shut the end of day.

The papers blow.

Old men, half-young again, across the
    pavements go

To cars that in imagination

Might this hour leave for Mars.

But, sons beside them silent, put in gear,

And drive off toward the close of one more year.

Both thinking this:

The game is done.

The game begins.

The game is lost.

But here come other wins.

The band tromps out to clear the field with
    brass,

The great heart of the drum systolic beats

In promise of yet greater feats and trumps;

Still promising, the band departs

To leave the final beating of this time

To older hearts who in the stands cold rinsed
    with Autumn day

Wish, want, desire for their sons

From here on down, eternal replay on replay.

This thought, them thinking it,

Man and boy, old Dad, raw Son

For one rare moment caused by cornering
    too fast,

Their shoulders lean and touch.

A red light stops them. Quiet and serene they sit.

But now the moment is past.

Gone is the day.

And so the old man says at last:

"The light is green, boy. Go. The light is green."

They ran together all the afternoon;

Now, very simply, they drive away.

Ray Bradbury

Descriptions of the Photographs

Most of the photographs in this book were made during the 1974 season by the seven photographers credited on the title page.

These men, each working in different geographic areas of the nation, attended NFL games with a very special purpose: to capture on film the sport of professional football as experienced by the players, coaches, and officials.

Each of the photographers worked with 35 mm. cameras, most equipped with a variety of lenses ranging from 17 mm. wide angle to 500 mm. telephoto. Utilizing this equipment with sensitivity, judgment, and obvious skill, they produced more than 20,000 exposures. The personal intensity and involvement of men caught up in the action of a sport may never have been as successfully documented.

To augment the work of the seven primary photographers, certain individual photographs were selected from the library of NFL Properties Creative Services. The photographers responsible are credited in the following descriptions.

Because of the special pride to detail that the photographers brought to their assignments, because of the faithful duotone filmwork produced by the technicians of Gardner/Fulmer Lithograph, and because of the fine printing of R. R. Donnelley and Sons, this book meets the high standards originally envisioned for it.

David Boss
June 26, 1975

Dust jacket cover: Rams' defensive end Fred Dryer rests on the sidelines during an intensely fought battle with the Vikings (Peter Read Miller).

Pages 10-11: The meticulously arranged dressing room of the visiting Chargers awaits the arrival of the players for a game in Denver's Mile High Stadium (Peter Read Miller).

Page 12: A hatrack full of Chargers' helmets (Peter Read Miller).

Page 13: As a teammate stretches, Chargers' receiver Gary Garrison awaits his turn on the trainer's table (Peter Read Miller).

Pages 14-15: Chargers' assistant trainer Jim Hammond deftly wraps an ankle (Peter Read Miller).

Pages 16-17: Fully dressed, except for shoulder pads, Cowboys' linebacker D. D. Lewis goes through some stretching exercises (Ross Lewis).

Page 18: With the game moments away, Cardinals' players slip into individual worlds of private contemplation (Herb Weitman).

Page 19a: Cardinals' linebacker Larry Stallings focuses his thoughts upon the immediate future (Herb Weitman).

Page 19b: Cardinals' assistant coach Sid Hall dictates some final instructions (Herb Weitman).

Pages 20-21: Cowboys' players climb the steps from their dressing room to begin a game with the New York Giants (Ross Lewis).

Page 22: The Redskins congregate at the head of the tunnel to await pregame introductions (Paul Fine).

Page 23: Cardinals' defensive end Council Rudolph stands patiently before the graffiti-covered wall of the Yale Bowl tunnel (Herb Weitman).

Page 24a: Redskins' guard Ray Schoenke stretches nervously as white-haired Bill John of the Rams prepares to introduce the offensive players to the crowd at the Los Angeles Coliseum. The ambulance, right, is a reminder of the dangers of the game about to begin (Peter Read Miller).

Page 24b: A huge American flag is stretched across the field at Pittsburgh's Three Rivers Stadium during pregame ceremonies (Ross Lewis).

Page 25: Cowboys' running back Walt Garrison (Ross Lewis).

Pages 26-27: A press box spotlight follows Rams' center Rich Saul as he is introduced at the Los Angeles Coliseum (Peter Read Miller).

Page 28: Under a bright November sun, captains of the Giants and Jets meet at midfield to re-enact the coin toss prior to the kickoff (Ross Lewis).

Pages 38-39: The camera captures the fluid throwing motion of Bengals' quarterback Ken Anderson (M. V. Rubio).

Pages 40-41: The elation of a last-second victory is demonstrated by Steelers' receiver Frank Lewis in a game at Busch Memorial Stadium in St. Louis (Herb Weitman).

Pages 42-43: Two Saints' defensive tackles, Derland Moore and Bob Pollard, wrestle Dolphins' running back Larry Csonka to the turf in Tulane Stadium (M.V. Rubio).

Pages 44-45: An August sunset lends a surrealistic mood to a field goal attempt in a preseason game between the Rams and Dolphins (Peter Read Miller).

Page 46: The clasped hands of a resting player (Peter Read Miller).

Pages 54-55: A Bills' lineman rests on the sideline, his pants covered with blood from a cut on his hand (Ross Lewis).

Page 56: An unidentified Patriot (Peter Read Miller).

Page 57: Raiders' tight end Warren Bankston grimaces in pain (Peter Read Miller).

Pages 58-59: A Bills' lineman sits quietly, helmet in hand, ready to return to the battle (Ross Lewis).

Page 60: Falcons' linebacker Tommy Nobis rests a bloodied hand on his battle-scarred helmet (Michael Zagaris).

Page 61: December raindrops bead on the plastic helmet of an Eagles' player (Ross Lewis).

Page 62: The massive hand of Raiders' tackle Art Shell is sheathed in a leather glove, reinforced with adhesive tape (Peter Read Miller).

Page 63: Redskins' safety Ken Houston wears a temporary bandage to shield a bruised cheekbone (Ross Lewis).

Page 64: Raiders' defensive end Horace Jones wipes away perspiration during a humid afternoon in Cleveland (Ross Lewis).

Page 65: The hands of an unidentified player (Herb Weitman).

Page 66: Chiefs' running back Ed Podolak ignores a bloodied nose (Rod Hanna).

Pages 76-77: The shadows of Patriots' players and coaches stretch across the artificial turf of Schaefer Stadium (Ross Lewis).

Page 78: The precise moment when toe meets ball. A new game is underway in Cincinnati (M.V. Rubio).

Page 79: The sideline chain gang, which controls the yard-line markers, watches as the ball is put into play (Peter Read Miller).

Page 80: The middle linebacker stands directly over the offensive center as two teams prepare for the snap of the ball (Herb Weitman).

Page 81: Chiefs' middle linebacker Willie Lanier (Rod Hanna).

Page 82: Lions' tackle Rockne Freitas (Tony Tomsic).

Page 83: Dolphins' center Jim Langer sets to protect quarterback Bob Griese (David Boss).

Page 84-85: With perfect coordination, 49ers' runners Wilbur Jackson and Larry Schreiber sprint from their set position (Herb Weitman).

Pages 86-87: In an explosion of human bodies, the front lines of the Broncos and Chiefs come together (Rod Hanna).

Page 88: Cardinals' defensive tackle Dave Butz fights off the double-team block of two Eagles' opponents (Herb Weitman).

Page 89: Chiefs' guard Ed Budde is 265 pounds of controlled power as he pulls to lead a runner downfield (Rod Hanna).

Pages 90-91: 49ers' center Forrest Blue and guard Woody Peoples shut off the rush of two Falcons' defenders, middle linebacker Tommy Nobis and defensive tackle Chuck Walker (M.V. Rubio).

Page 92: Rams' running back Lawrence McCutcheon (Rob Meneilly).

Page 93: Colts' middle linebacker Mike Curtis battles Falcons' center Jeff Van Note one-on-one as he fights his way to the ball carrier (M.V. Rubio).

Page 94: Cowboys' runner Walt Garrison challenges Cardinals' defenders Larry Stallings and Bob Rowe (Herb Weitman).

Page 95: The Redskins' Ken Houston and Pat Fischer team up to stop Eagles' running back Norm Bulaich (M.V. Rubio).

Page 96: Raiders' running back Clarence Davis disappears under a surging wave of Chargers' tacklers, including linebacker Carl Gersbach (James F. Flores).

Page 97: Referee Chuck Heberling takes the ball as players unpile after the play in a Giants-Jets game (Ross Lewis).

Page 98: Cowboys' coach Tom Landry (Ross Lewis).

Page 99: Eagles' coach Mike McCormack (Ross Lewis).

Page 100: Rams' running back Lawrence McCutcheon (David Boss).

Page 101: 49ers' middle linebacker Frank Nunley (M.V. Rubio).

Pages 102-103: 49ers' passing coach Don Heinrich gives receiver Danny Abramowicz a play to take onto the field (Michael Zagaris).

Page 104: Back judge Hugh (Sonny) Gamber indicates third down (Ross Lewis).

Pages 112-113: As the Raiders' gather for an offensive huddle, guard Gene Upshaw (63) looks over the Dolphins' defense (Peter Read Miller).

Page 114: Chiefs' linebacker Bobby Bell (Malcolm Emmons).

Page 115: The Bills huddle in their own end zone (M.V. Rubio).

Pages 116-117: The strength and power of an offensive guard is captured in this portrait of the Lions' Chuck Walton (George Gellatly).

Page 118: Bears' running back Carl Garrett blocks Vikings' defensive end Jim Marshall (Malcolm Emmons).

Page 119: Falcons' defensive end John Zook is caught in a 49ers' double-team block as tackle Len Rohde shoves him backward over the fallen tight end, Tom Mitchell (M. V. Rubio).

Page 120: Agile as dancers, the Dolphins' 252-pound defensive end Bill Stanfill and 220-pound middle linebacker Nick Buoniconti leap to defend against the Saints (M. V. Rubio).

Page 121: Jets' guard Gary Puetz fires out at Giants' defensive tackle Gary Pettigrew (Ross Lewis).

Pages 122-123: Rams' runner Lawrence McCutcheon is dwarfed behind the massive wall of his offensive linemen as they seal off the defending 49ers (James F. Flores).

Page 124-125: 49ers' power runner Larry Schreiber dives head-first into the ruck of the scrimmage. Falcons' defensive end Claude Humphrey (87) and middle linebacker Tommy Nobis make the tackle (M. V. Rubio).

Pages 126-127: Cardinals' defensive tackle Bob Rowe puts a headlock on Redskins' runner Duane Thomas (Herb Weitman).

Page 128: Umpire Paul Trepinski calls for the ball (Ross Lewis).

Page 129: Chiefs' middle linebacker Willie Lanier (Rod Hanna).

Page 130: Dolphins' center Jim Langer's hand grips the ball (M. V. Rubio).

Page 131: 49ers' linebacker Dave Wilcox (David Boss).

Pages 132-133: Falcons' defensive end Claude Humphrey (M. V. Rubio).

Pages 134-135: Bengals' defensive tackle Mike Reid fights off 49ers' guard Woody Peoples in an effort to reach running back Wilbur Jackson (Michael Zagaris).

Pages 136-137: Vikings' running back Dave Osborn blocks for Chuck Foreman (44) (Herb Weitman).

Page 138: Eagles' middle linebacker Bill Bergey is knocked head-over-heels (Herb Weitman).

Page 139: Cartwheeling gracefully, 49ers' running back Wilbur Jackson appears as weightless as an astronaut as he picks up yardage against the Falcons (M. V. Rubio).

Pages 140-141: Seemingly startled by his predicament, Cowboys' quarterback Roger Staubach comes to rest under the weight of Cardinals' defenders Bob Bell and Ron Yankowski (Herb Weitman).

Page 142: Rams' head coach Chuck Knox (James F. Flores).

Page 143: A Chargers' assistant coach holds a drawing of pass routes for his players (Peter Read Miller).

Pages 144-145: The Steelers' offensive team breaks huddle (M. V. Rubio).

Page 146: Raiders' wide receiver Mike Siani (Herb Weitman).

Page 147: Cardinals' cornerback Roger Wehrli (Herb Weitman).

Page 148: Driving hard but seemingly without effort, Oilers' wide receiver Ken Burrough begins his pass pattern (Herb Weitman).

Page 149: Wearing a smile, Falcons' cornerback Rolland Lawrence heads toward the action (M. V. Rubio).

Page 150: Exploding backward, Ron Yary, the Vikings' powerful tackle, sets to pass block (David Boss).

Page 151: Falcons' guard Jim Miller and center Jeff Van Note double-team Cowboys' defensive tackle Bill Gregory (M. V. Rubio).

Pages 152-153: With 6-foot 6-inch, 240-pound defensive end Roy Hilton of the Giants bearing down on him, Jets' quarterback Joe Namath stands his ground (Ross Lewis).

Pages 154-155: In an all-out effort, 49ers' receiver Danny Abramowicz stretches for the ball (Michael Zagaris).

Page 156: Pummeled from the left and right by Rams' linebackers Ken Geddes and Jack Reynolds, 49ers' tight end Tom Mitchell hangs onto a pass (Michael Zagaris).

Page 157: Vikings' receiver John Gilliam is the victim of tackle by Steelers' middle linebacker Jack Lambert (M. V. Rubio).

Pages 158-159: Water sprays from the AstroTurf surface of Riverfront Stadium as Cardinals' linebacker Pete Barnes smothers a Bengals' receiver (Herb Weitman).

Page 160: Steelers' safety Glen Edwards (Peter Read Miller).

Page 161: His jersey in tatters, Browns' running back Greg Pruitt heads for the bench for repairs in a game against the Chargers in San Diego (James F. Flores).

Page 162: Browns' defensive tackle Walter Johnson finds comfort in a clean towel on the bench (James F. Flores).

Page 163a: A pair of Jets rest on the bench at Shea Stadium (Ross Lewis).

Page 163b: An oxygen bottle (Ross Lewis).

Page 164a: A towel dipped in ice water brings relief to Cardinals' tackle Dan Dierdorf (Herb Weitman).

Page 164b: Dolphins' tight end Jim Mandich (Ross Lewis).

Page 165a: Cleveland Browns' safety Thom Darden (Ross Lewis).

Page 165b: A much-handled, plastic squeeze bottle (Ross Lewis).

Pages 166-167: Raiders' tackle Art Shell squeezes off a refreshing shot of Gatorade (Peter Read Miller).

Page 168: An injured player sits with his teammates on the Saints' bench (M. V. Rubio).

Page 169a: A trainer examines the eye of 49ers' receiver Danny Abramowicz (Bob McGregor).

Page 169b: A comforting hand assures a Colts' player during a game with the Jets (Ross Lewis).

Pages 170-171: Packers' defensive end Alden Roche (Ross Lewis).

Pages 172-173: Cardinals' running back Terry Metcalf is disconsolate as he sits out the remainder of a game, his bruised knee wrapped in an ice pack (Herb Weitman).

Page 174: Bears' linebacker Waymond Bryant (M. V. Rubio).

Page 175: Patriots' running back Sam Cunningham holds a fistful of guard John Hannah's jersey on a run against Buffalo (Dick Raphael).

Page 176: A four-photo sequence shows the acceleration of Packers' running back John Brockington as he cuts up the sideline and races by the Cardinals' defenders, tackle Bob Rowe and cornerback Roger Wehrli (Herb Weitman).

Page 177: Raiders' running back Marv Hubbard attempts to pull away from Chargers' defensive end Dave Tipton (Peter Read Miller).

Page 178: Broncos' running back Floyd Little (Rod Hanna).

Page 179: Eagles' linebackers Steve Zabel and Bill Bergey swarm over Redskins' running back Moses Denson (M. V. Rubio).

Page 180: Cardinals' running back Terry Metcalf is caught in the vise of Chiefs' cornerback Jim Marsalis and defensive end Marvin Upshaw (Herb Weitman).

Page 181a: The heart of the Vikings' defense watches with interest as team physician Dr. Donald Lannin, left, and trainer Fred Zamberletti attend unconscious linebacker Amos Martin (James F. Flores).

Page 181b: Dazed Steelers' safety Mike Wagner is guided from the field by team physician Dr. John Best, trainer Ralph Berlin, and assistant trainer Bob Milie (Ross Lewis).

Page 182: Redskins' running back Herb Mul-Key is treated for a shoulder separation by team physician Dr. P. M. Palumbo, Jr. (Ross Lewis).

Page 183: Jets' linebacker Ralph Baker cries out in pain as a broken finger on his left hand is treated (Ross Lewis).

Page 184: Rams' defensive end Fred Dryer and tackle Merlin Olsen (Peter Read Miller).

Page 185: Browns' defensive end Allen Aldridge head tackles Cardinals' running back Ken Willard (Herb Weitman).

Page 186: Saints' runner Jess Phillips attempts to leap over a pile of bodies at the line, but Dolphins' safety Dick Anderson repels him with a well-directed elbow (M. V. Rubio).

Page 187: The ball is only scant inches off the fingers of Falcons' receiver Ken Burrow; 49ers' cornerback Ralph McGill views the miss with pleasure (M. V. Rubio).

Page 188a: Two Falcons, quarterback Bob Lee and running back Eddie Ray, protest a judgment call vehemently, but head linesman Tony Veteri calmly ignores them (M. V. Rubio).

Page 188b: 49ers' receiver Danny Abramowicz argues loudly with referee John McDonough (Michael Zagaris).

Page 189: Redskins' coach George Allen makes a pointed statement about the officiating to back judge Gordon McCarter and umpire Paul Trepinski. Assistant coach Charlie Waller is a dour supporter (Ross Lewis).

Pages 190-191: On a bleak winter's day in St. Louis, quarterback Jim Hart sinks to his knees during the Cardinals' loss to the Chiefs (Herb Weitman).

Page 192: Raiders' guard Gene Upshaw begins to strip the wrappings from his arms as a game against San Diego nears its end. Wide receiver Mike Siani stands nearby (James F. Flores).

Pages 200-201: The lights of Philadelphia's Veterans Stadium fuse with a December drizzle to create a dramatic backdrop for a game between the Eagles and Packers (Ross Lewis).

Pages 202-203: The Redskins' offensive team forms its huddle during a late Sunday afternoon game against the Cowboys (Ross Lewis).

Pages 204-205: Eager for play to begin, quarterback Bert Jones smacks his hands together in the Colts' huddle during a time out against the Jets (Ross Lewis).

Page 206: The electronic message board at Busch Memorial Stadium in St. Louis (Herb Weitman).

Page 207: The legs of Broncos' running back Floyd Little (David Boss).

Page 208: Bears' receiver George Farmer (Herb Weitman).

Page 209: Casting a suspicious eye toward the offense, Dolphins' safety Dick Anderson sizes up the strategy (David Boss).

Page 210: Raiders' guard George Buehler meets the rush of the St. Louis front four (Herb Weitman).

Page 211: Sprinting downfield, 6-foot 5-inch Jets' wide receiver Richard Caster makes a superb target (Ross Lewis).

Page 212: With the Raiders' 265-pound defensive end, Bubba Smith, attacking him from behind, Jets' quarterback Joe Namath passes (Russ Reed).

Page 213: A thoughtful moment consumes the Raiders' usually animated and vocal coach, John Madden (Peter Read Miller).

Pages 214-215: The end zone is a carnival ground of graffiti as Raiders' wide receiver Cliff Branch scores against the Dolphins. Field judge Jimmy Cole gives the touchdown signal (Michael Zagaris).

Page 216: The Chiefs' Otis Taylor soars high to spike the football in the end zone after completing a touchdown play (Rod Hanna).

Page 217: The 49ers join in an end zone celebration of a score in a game against the Raiders. Shown are tackle Cas Banaszek (79), center Forrest Blue (75), receiver Danny Abramowicz (46), running backs Sammy Williams (24) and Manfred Moore (45), and guard John Watson (67) (Michael Zagaris).

Pages 218-219: Rams' linebacker Ken Geddes is unrestrained in his joy of an interception that saved a victory against the Vikings. Center Rich Saul, equipment manager Don Hewitt, safety Steve Preece, and defensive tackle Phil Olsen greet him enthusiastically (Peter Read Miller).

Pages 220-221: Bills' running back O. J. Simpson is a forlorn figure on an empty bench near the end of a playoff defeat to the Steelers (Ross Lewis).

Page 222: An unidentified Eagle shields himself beneath his parka from December's gloom (Ross Lewis).

Page 223: Steelers' defensive end Dwight White is alive with the elation of an AFC championship victory over the Raiders (Peter Read Miller).

Page 224: A single tear marks the deep disappointment felt by Bills' wide receiver Ahmad Rashad as the season ends in defeat (Robert L. Smith).

Page 225: Raiders' linebacker Phil Villapiano is emotionally overcome by the Raiders' last-moment win over the Dolphins in an AFC playoff game (Peter Read Miller).

Pages 226-227: An intense game between the Redskins and the Dolphins that was not decided until the final seconds resulted in this emotional reaction from winning coach George Allen (Ross Lewis).

Pages 228-229: Steelers' running back Franco Harris and defensive tackle Joe Greene give their coach, Chuck Noll, a victory ride from the field of Super Bowl IX, where Pittsburgh won its first NFL championship by defeating Minnesota (M. V. Rubio).

Page 230: Raiders' tight end Bob Moore is engulfed by Oakland fans at the end of a game (Peter Read Miller).

Page 231: Bills' quarterback Joe Ferguson congratulates Steelers' quarterback Terry Bradshaw following a divisional playoff game (M. V. Rubio).

Pages 232-233: Rams' center Ken Iman walks from the field with his son following a playoff victory over the Washington Redskins (Peter Read Miller).

Pages 234-235: Chargers' cornerback Bob Howard (24) and safety Joe Beauchamp (40) walk from the field to a chorus of taunts by Raiders' fans. Raiders' defensive tackle Otis Sistrunk (60) is an impervious victor (Peter Read Miller).

Pages 236-237: The blinding glare of television lights greets the Raiders as they climb the steps to the post-game dressing room (Peter Read Miller).

Pages 238-239: Savoring the experience of a divisional championship, Cardinals' coach Don Coryell (foreground) and running backs Terry Metcalf and Ken Willard celebrate happily (Herb Weitman).

Page 240: The bearer of a split lip, wide receiver J. V. Cain is stitched by Cardinals' physicians Dr. James C. Ellsasser (right) and Dr. Charles L. Roper (Herb Weitman).

Page 241: Eddie Alexander of KRON-TV, San Francisco, interviews Raiders' running back Marv Hubbard (Peter Read Miller).

Page 242: Raiders' cornerback Nemiah Wilson huddles in a corner of the Raiders' dressing room following a bitter loss to the Steelers in the AFC championship game (Peter Read Miller).

Page 243: The hands of an unidentified Bills' player (Ross Lewis).

Pages 244-245: With evening approaching, the gulls from nearby San Francisco Bay swoop low over the empty cavern of the Oakland-Alameda County Coliseum (Peter Read Miller).

Dust jacket back cover: Steelers' quarterback Terry Bradshaw passes against the Vikings in Super Bowl IX (M. V. Rubio).